Priest in New York

Priest in New York

Church, Street, and Theology

Victor Lee Austin

Foreword by Jon Meacham

Saint Thomas Church Fifth Avenue
New York

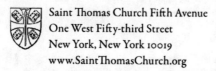 Saint Thomas Church Fifth Avenue
One West Fifty-third Street
New York, New York 10019
www.SaintThomasChurch.org

First edition 2010
ISBN: 978-0-578-07107-7
Library of Congress Control Number: 2010939271

To Nancy and Susan
who walk

Contents

Acknowledgments

Writing is an act committed in solitude for the sake of others. To help me move my words out of their initial solitude into print I have had the benefit of many friends, two of whom deserve special thanks. At a crucial juncture in this project, Linda Bridges helped me realize its overall shape. And Heather Cross has brought competence and patient attention to the design and production of this book. You would not be reading this, had it not been for them.

This book is something of a sequel to *A Priest's Journal*, which was written while I was rector of the Church of the Resurrection in Hopewell Junction, New York. When the Reverend Andrew C. Mead called me to be theologian-in-residence of Saint Thomas Church, it was part of his hope for me and for the church that there would be another "priest's journal." I am grateful to him for his vision and his continuing trust.

"Ashes," "Avery," "Awesomeness," "Cookbooks," "Do You Still Have a Job?," "Night," "Senior Coffee," and "Waiting Room" previously appeared in *The Anglican*. "We Don't Know How to Pray" previously appeared, under a different title, in *The Living Church*. I extend my thanks to the editors of those publications.

Some names herein are pseudonyms.

Foreword

In one of Dorothy Sayers's Peter Wimsey mysteries, the author has her hero, on hearing the sound of bells, remark, "Where is a church, there is civilization." This is not always true—history is rife with examples of uncivilized behavior by ecclesiastical figures—but the point remains a good one. The bells of the Christian church ring out in times of grief and joy, of commemoration and communion. Some of them also ring the time, marking with precision the passing of the hours of this world and reminding hearers of the world to come. In the shadows of churches, we are, then, constantly aware of the dichotomy of human existence and the mystery of pilgrimage—that we on earth are not finally home, for home lies beyond time and beyond space, in what Jesus calls his father's "many mansions."

And yet our eyes and hearts cannot be solely focused on the hereafter, for we are charged with making gentle the life of the here and now. Such is the work of all Christians, but it is the particular province of those in holy orders, the deacons, priests, and bishops who stand in the long succession that began in an upper room in a Jerusalem spring around the year 30 AD.

In the Anglican tradition, priests are called to be, in the words of the 1928 Book of Common Prayer, "Messengers, Watchmen, and Stewards of the Lord"; they are directed, moreover, to "teach, and to premonish, to feed and provide for the Lord's family; to seek for Christ's sheep that are dispersed abroad, and for his children who are in the midst of this naughty world, that they may be saved through Christ forever."

Noble language, and epic sentiments. The significance and value of Victor Austin's following account of life as a priest in New York City is his capacity to make the challenges and joys of teaching and, yes, premonishing (a lovely word, that) real to us without descending into cynicism or sensationalism. This is a quiet book about a loud city, a faithful diary of a world too often given to faithlessness.

Father Austin lives and moves and has his being in a beautiful parish, an architectural gem that more than meets the test of a church to be an icon of the New Jerusalem. And every day, the bells of Saint Thomas Church Fifth Avenue ring the hours, and the sanctus bells commemorate the keeping of Jesus' commandment to "Do this in remembrance of Me." The notes ring out over Fifth Avenue and around midtown Manhattan, an island devoted to what Wordsworth called the getting and spending of the world. But in their sound there is a reminder of the church of God and the civilization of men.

This book is a kind of bell, and its sound, too, evokes the eternal and the temporal, and in Father Austin's words and deeds we are reminded anew that Lord Wimsey was on to something: where is a church, there is indeed civilization—so long as the church is served by priests of grace and good will. You are about to meet such a priest in the following pages.

Jon Meacham

2010

Priest in New York

Scrambling After Jesus

IN THE TRADITIONAL ANGLICAN LITURGY, there are scripture sentences said right after the confession and absolution. These sentences are commonly called the Comfortable Words, the first one of which is this: *Come unto me, all ye that travail and are heavy laden, and I will give you rest*. But who is this Jesus who offers rest? He seems to be always on the move.

Within just the first chapter of Mark, a series of very short vignettes establish Jesus as a man of power striding across the Galilean stage. Jesus sees fishermen—Simon and Andrew, then James and John—and tells them to follow him. They do so at once. Jesus enters the synagogue on the Sabbath and teaches. Everyone feels the power of his teaching. A man who was possessed by a demon comes up to him, and Jesus liberates him, driving the demon away. Jesus leaves the synagogue and goes to the home of Simon and Andrew. Simon's mother-in-law is there, struck down by a fever. Jesus heals her. As soon as the sun sets—which is to say, at their first opportunity—all the people of the city come to the house where Jesus is, bringing the sick and the possessed. Jesus performs many miracles of healing and liberation. Then in the dark, very early in the morning, Jesus goes out into the wilderness to pray. There his disciples find him, having gone out in search of him;

they tell him that everyone in the city is looking for him. But Jesus says he must go on to all the other towns also. It turns out that Jesus had left before sunrise in order, not to go out to pray—although he did pray and prayer was undoubtedly important—but because only long before dawn would he be able to escape the people of that town.

Teaching, healing, and liberation from demonic possession: this is the powerful work that Jesus does as he strides from shore to synagogue to house and from town to town. And by doing so, everyone is drawn to him. Some he calls, like Andrew, Simon, James and John, and they become his disciples. Others, the crowds, are drawn to him. And what they receive from him gives them, we might say, something like immediate satisfaction. The teaching right away is seen as authentic and powerful; the healing and the liberation is manifested at once. This is of course a highly agreeable situation, and it is no wonder that the whole city would come to his door, the whole district come out even just to touch the fringe of his garment. Jesus gave them something they wanted, and it was very good.

But his disciples, those four men at this point, their call is to follow him. And it is not a call to follow him only at the beginning, but to keep following him. And it is not particularly easy to follow Jesus. They go with him to synagogue; they bring him to their home; they presumably try to manage and assist with the crowd. But then they wake up…and he's gone! They have to scramble after him; they don't know where he is; when at last they catch up with him, he says he is moving on, going out to other towns and cities, walking down additional roads. To follow Jesus is not to rest, not to stay at ease, but to be pulled along, taken into the country and to places where one might never have gone.

How can we hold together this picture of Jesus, the Jesus of power and magnetism who is, let's face it, working very hard, with the picture of Jesus who offers rest to the weary? *Come unto me*, that Jesus said, *and I will give you rest*. The crowds get their immediate satisfactions, while the disciples have to scramble after, never quite keeping up with Jesus, never able to claim that cessation of labor that we call rest.

And we know where it is going to lead. Those disciples will follow him to an end that will come far too soon. They will run away, and from a human point of view it all will end quite tragically. It seems not only work to follow Jesus, but heartbreak.

Some of my readers may be feeling acutely the financial uncertainty of our time. Others may feel the personal uncertainty that is characteristic of all time. We may be confused; we may confront serious illness; we may be heavily burdened by forces outside our control. What Jesus offers us is a complex remedy. On the one hand, there is the immediate satisfaction that he truly gives, and that perhaps each of us has experienced at some time: the clarity of his thought, the healing of his touch, the peace that passeth understanding. On the other hand, there is the call to follow after him: which is, seemingly, a call to perpetual motion, to rising early and going to bed late, to facing the crowds and then going to meet new ones. But that, too, is peace and rest; that activity of Jesus is itself peace and rest. For the problem (I believe) is in our conception of what it means to be given rest. We think of "rest" as the cessation of motion, as a stopping of activity, as something like sleep. But God's rest is not like what we think of as rest. God's rest is just one human and inadequate way of talking about God's being. God's rest, God's being, is ever-creative, always supporting the universe in being, always giving health and freedom and truth.

To participate in Jesus' activity is to participate in God's being, and that, in a totally surprising way, turns out to be God's rest.

I bet if we asked Jesus' disciples if they were tired or weary when they were going around with him and chasing after him and all that happened during the years of Jesus' ministry on earth, I bet if we asked them, they would say to us that they were never for one minute weary. They were working longer weeks than any of us, and yet, because it was Jesus' work—God's work—that they were doing, they were not for one second weary. That, too, is the peace that passeth understanding.

We Don't Know How to Pray

I THINK THAT PEOPLE TEND to think of priests as being "prayer professionals." Just as we expect an accountant to be expert in finance and a solicitor to be expert in law, so we might expect clergy to be experts in prayer. And I think, correspondingly, a lot of clergy feel like imposters who carry about a dark secret they must work to keep covered up. At least, when it comes to prayer, I feel like an imposter. I don't have interesting or moving "spiritual" experiences. I don't spend a lot of time in prayer on my knees, or even on my rear end. Yet I do teach about prayer. And even as I do so, I wonder if I'm unwittingly fulfilling the old prophecy that those who can, do, and those who can't…

But perhaps the problem of prayer is at the same time the blessing. Herbert McCabe starts one of his talks on prayer by quoting Saint Paul, who says in his letter to the Romans (8:26) that *we do not know how to pray*. McCabe underlines that Paul is stating that he, the great Saint Paul, does not know how to pray. And that, McCabe says, has got to be good news for us. Perhaps it is impossible for us to know how to pray, impossible, that is, to comprehend what happens in prayer. There are famously difficult questions about prayer. How it is possible for me, a creature, to talk to God, my creator? Why does God need me to

5

speak to him since, being God, he already knows everything? If God is eternal and unchanging and thus not in time, how could he change his mind and do something as a result of my praying? And these are just a few of the questions which, when you start to think about them, you realize you don't have a chance in understanding. In fact, as we say, you don't have a prayer.

With regard to prayer, what we need to do is just do it. Simon Tugwell is good on this point. There need be nothing unusual about prayer, nothing esoteric or mysterious. You just talk to God, asking him for whatever you want to ask him. It doesn't need to be long to be prayer; in fact, a few seconds are enough. It also doesn't have to be silent. You need no particular posture. Ask him to help your mother. Ask him to take care of your friend in San Antonio. Ask him for the money you need. Ask him for whatever you really want.

I think a lot of prayer, perhaps all of prayer, is simply a matter of being mindful that I am living my life with God. He holds me in being continually, and he is closer to me than my next heartbeat. What happens to me is, say, I find it's the middle of the afternoon and I haven't been able to write much all day. And then I realize I haven't been speaking with God. So I say to him, "God, what I'd really like this afternoon is to write a chapter for my priest's journal book." And at that moment I think: I could write a chapter on prayer.

What one hopes for is to have those periods of forgetfulness become shorter. I don't expect them ever to disappear, and I suppose there might actually be more of them. Often with regard to God it seems that any step forward is accompanied by many impulses to turn away. But the forgetful times can get shorter as the moments of recollection become more frequent. God is with me as I walk this busy city, as I pass the sexy ads, pass the beautiful people, and the poor people, and the fruit vendors, and the sidewalk washers, and even the man who jerks and slaps and thrusts out the Flash Dancer cards. God holds me in existence, as he holds all them in existence.

So I can ask him. What do I really want? Sometimes what I really want is for the city's cruelty and human manipulation to come to an end. And sometimes all I want is to get in out of the summer heat. In church, sometimes I hope the liturgy will be beautiful and the people will find themselves longing for God. And sometimes all I want is for the liturgy to be over so I can sit down.

I don't know how to pray. But I can ask him.

Walking

MY OKLAHOMA RELATIVES couldn't believe it when I told them I'd be selling my car before moving to New York. They asked, "How will you live without a car? How will you go shopping?"

"We'll walk," I said cheerfully. "New Yorkers do a lot of walking."

Susan, my wife, had broken her hip during Holy Week a few years before our move. That, on top of her earlier treatments for a brain tumor, has left her with difficulty walking, but she thinks positively about it. We walk more slowly than most people, her cane clutched in her right hand while her left hangs onto my elbow. The sidewalks can be crowded. There are treacherous unevennesses in the surface; there are pushy people who seem oblivious to the danger they pose to frail walkers. Susan won't go out alone, but despite the difficulties she likes being out.

She sees things that I don't see when I'm walking alone—alas, I'm too often one of those pushy walkers. Susan sees with delight the variety of folks who are out. She sees the gnarled trees and the black squirrels of Central Park. She sees babies, and dogs, and joggers, and sports teams. And she sees the homeless.

We turn the corner from our apartment onto Seventh Avenue, and there, sitting on a plastic crate by the never-used payphone, is a man rattling a cup asking passersby for change. He says the same thing to everyone—except to Susan. "How are you, little lady?" he says, and she stops to turn her face to him. She is smiling.

There is a saxophone player on 57th Street; she wants to give him some money. (She never gives money except to musicians.) Down around 55th Street she smiles at the man sitting in a wheelchair; he pauses his normal chatter to greet her.

It's not that they know each other, these panhandlers and homeless people and my wife. It's that they recognize something in each other, something they have in common.

Once we were walking home from MOMA, bundled for the cold. As we finished crossing the street, Susan tripped on the curb. It is for me the stuff of nightmare, played out in slow motion. Her body starts to fall; her hand slips a bit in my arm; she twists; the cane clanks on the concrete; I hear her head make its thunk. This time she has landed on her back and indeed it was a slow fall. I thank God she is conscious—I remember earlier falls, and concussions, and the broken hip.

"Little sister, are you all right? Are you all right?" The voice came from a man sitting at the corner by the building. He had a cup in his hand, a cup he was still shaking. You could hear the coins clinking against each other, but he had stopped his repetitious asking for change. Instead he was saying, was repeating over and over, "Are you all right?"

She was. I helped her up, and she brushed her coat down, took her cane from me, took my arm, and turned to him. "Yes, I'm all right," she said.

Awesomeness

A NEW PRIEST, I took my senior high youth on a weekend retreat to a conference center in the Adirondack mountains. It was winter. Around us were evergreen trees, snowy fields, and a frozen lake right beside the house. On Sunday morning we were walking through this pristine and cold environment, the low-sky sun hitting our eyes not only from above but from everywhere it could be reflected off the snow. Cheryl said something that stuck. "I never feel close to God in church. But here—here is where I can feel God."

It was, I think, a sense of the immensity of God's creative accomplishment that she was feeling. For many of us something happens in nature. The view from the top of a mountain, or the vast ocean stretching before us seemingly to infinity, or lying on the grass at night under a million quivering stars: these are the moments when we feel true awe, when we draw close to the maker of the universe. We don't feel the awesomeness of things in our quotidian life because the parameters of our vision are set within the range of human-sized things. But catch the sight of the very large—the mountain, the sea, the sky—and we are reminded that the world is vast beyond any possibility of our grasping it.

And that's a good thing to remember, for we are made-beings, we are creatures, and what it means to be a creature is that you can never get your hands around your creator; indeed, you can't even get your mind around him. Who could swallow the ocean? Who could replicate Mount Marcy? Who could travel to all the stars? Yet even if you could do those things, you would still be no closer to the one who made them. The creator occupies no place in the creation.

With such thoughts our mind looks toward the abyss, trying to catch a glimpse of the hand that made it and never succeeding, but feeling that which it is appropriate for a creature to feel, feeling awe. Awe is our proper stance toward our creator.

City dwellers may be at a disadvantage here. We don't routinely experience the ocean (although it is not that far away, it is somehow different when the city abuts it with buildings, crowds, and trash). We would have to travel and hike to get to mountains. And we put out too much light to be able to see the stars. So it is hard for us to appreciate viscerally the awe of creation.

But God has not, as it were, left us without consolations. There is another doctrine of the faith that is, I think, easier for city-dwellers to contemplate: the awesome scope of God's redemptive intention. If the doctrine of creation tells us that God made absolutely everything, the doctrine of redemption tells us that God wants to bring salvation to absolutely everybody. And if the thought of God making the immeasurable reaches of the universe brings you to the feeling of awe, the thought that God desires to save every human being must also bring awe to those of us who live in a city of eight million.

The numbers are impossible to grasp. It is a thought both humbling and exhilarating to contemplate God's desire to save even just me. Then to look at the dozen folks at a weekday chapel mass and to think God wants to save all of them: it is a huge thought. It means God knows each of their lives intimately. He knows their history, their thoughts, their capacities; he also knows the sins that they are prone to and the impediments that surround them at home and at work and through society, impediments that keep them from being fully what he wants. And God intends to take their sins away, not (only) in the superficial or juridical sense that he will take their parking tickets and mark them "paid in full" so that they won't be guilty, but he intends to change their proneness to sin, and to change the sin that affects home and corporation and society, so that they will be transformed by him into the unique person they were always meant to be (and in some way already are, but not yet fulfilled). That's what the doctrine of the redemption means. And for him to do it just for those few people at mass is itself awesome. But God's intentions don't end there. Redemption is to extend to the seven hundred people who are at Saint Thomas on a Sunday. It extends to the five or ten thousand people who exit the midtown subway station across the street during the morning rush. It extends to the hundreds I might pass on the sidewalk on the way to church without giving them a thought. Everyone in every office building, everyone in all the city boroughs: God knows each one intimately and has saving designs for them all.

I'm all for the experience of the awesomeness of nature. God is the creator, and it's good to be caused to reflect on that. But if you want to experience awe at the unfathomable vastness of God's power, all you need to do is contemplate the millions that we work and live among, and think: Jesus died for all of these—all of us.

Ballet and the Soul

M Y DAUGHTER, EMILY, says that ballet is the most perfect of the fine arts. It is, first, like a painting, a visual field that is received contemporaneously, all at once. Of course paintings have parts, and tensions, and often a visual dynamic which intensifies as you ponder them. But the initial experience is a Gestalt, and ballet is visual in that way.

But it also has music. And music is a whole which exists at no particular moment, but which is stretched out over time. Music is, in that sense, the opposite of a painting; while paintings present us with the whole at once, music never gives us the whole, but requires of us an attentiveness stretched over time. Ballet combines these two fine arts; it is like a painting that moves to music. It has the wholeness of the spatial together with the wholeness of the temporal. And I think it provides a clue for how we can think of the soul, heaven, and God.

Consider first a deceptively simple question, "Where is a melody?" We all know the experience of having a terrible advertising jingle stuck in our minds; a few weeks ago, the old "I'd like to buy the world a Coke" (which is hardly as bad as most jingles) was annoyingly in my thoughts, unbidden and unwanted. But what do we mean when we say it's "in our minds"? I think we mean that somehow we are able to call up the music and think it through, imagine it being performed from beginning to end. It's in our memory like a vinyl on a turntable, just waiting for the needle to come down and actualize it.

I think what this means is that a melody, or indeed any musical composition, does not exist anywhere, although some sort of representation of it can exist (a chunk of memory, a vinyl disk, notes in ink on lined paper). The music itself, however, only exists while it is being played. But even that is not a complete answer: the music exists, while it is being played *and at the same time* while it is being attended to, by a mind that is capable of holding the passing sounds in its memory.

Conversely we could ask, "When does a painting exist?" And I think we would have to give a similar answer. A painting exists in no particular time. It is in a place, but it does not need the passing of time to exist. That is to say a painting exists in the timeless "now" that needs no duration. A good painting can be contemplated for hours, yet nonetheless in just a twinkling of an eye it can be taken in.

For the questions where is a melody and when is a painting, ballet suggests itself as an answer. Ballet gives a time over which the visual art exists, and a place within which the temporal art exists. In doing those two things it is like the ensouled human being. To say where a person exists is like asking where music exists: a person is a living body, and so he exists only over time, only in activity. (If there is no activity, there is no life.) The soul is the actualization of the body, its living-ness; dead things, soulless things, cannot move but can only be moved.

Each of us, I mean to say, is like a painting set to music. We exist when and where the dance is happening. What then of our life after death? When the body is placed in the grave, how can it dance? And where then is its soul? Whenever I teach a class on the Christian hope, it's always asked: Will heaven be interesting? Or won't it be a rather dull business, just singing all the time? Such questions leave the body out, and they usually think of a dead person as an immortal soul. But if a human person is body and soul together, and if *that* is something like a ballet—a time that holds the visual and a space that holds the temporal—then heaven can hardly be dull. For we won't be immortal souls only: we will be resurrected bodies, the whole person animated by God's Spirit. In the Christian destiny of resurrected bodies there is a lot more to do than just sing, although our singing will be infinitely more exciting than any song we have ever known this side of the grave. We will be able to be fully creative as we've never been before, uninhibited by jealousies and quarrels and all those things which hold us back so often. The resurrected life will be an explosion of creativity, the complete enjoyment of visual time and temporal space. The world to come cannot but be an active place, a place of continual novelty and delight, a time of ever-new music, ever-new performances.

The kingdom of heaven is where ballet is at home, the highest of all things.

Alleluia Man

UNSHAVEN, SKIN DRAWN, with fidgety hands, Peter sits towards the front of the chapel at many of our daily masses. Early on I found myself distracted during my homilies by his nervous squirming about. He leans forward, moves back, picks up the service card, shakes it, bends it, turns to the side. I will learn that his voice is hoarse, continually so.

At the end of mass I go to the back of the chapel to shake hands. "My name's Peter," the deep but scratchy voice said; "what's yours?" I told him as we shook hands, and at once he added, "Pray for me, Father, that I give up cigarettes."

And so we settled into our pattern. I say mass, he squirms; I greet him at the door. "Peace, Peter," I say; and he is pleased I remember his name. "Pray for me, Father—those cigarettes. I have to give them up." Sometimes it's a little different. Once he told me he hadn't smoked for three days. Once, that he hadn't smoked for five hours.

Jonathan (who was our youth minister and my office neighbor) usually would take the Tuesday healing mass. I ask him if he knows Peter. "He's always here," he says. I ask, half-grinning, "Have you healed him of his cigarette addiction?" Jonathan is very conscientious, and he has been known to spend more time in the back of the chapel after mass than he spent doing the whole service. When I see him Tuesday afternoons—it's often nearly two o'clock before he gets back to his office from the 12:10 mass, and he *hasn't yet had lunch*—I ask him how he's doing with healing the sick and raising the dead. But for Peter, I learn, Jonathan has a straight-forward and consistent line. To the request, "Pray for me, Father," Jonathan tells him, "Quit buying them."

Yet it seems Peter can't quit buying them. If even just a few hours go by without a smoke, he feels a great accomplishment and at the same time a terrible need. The man is in the grip of something much stronger than himself. One suspects he has tried many things. One fears that his days are nearing their end.

Still, something else also has a grip upon him. I have mentioned his voice. When I place the Bread in his hands and say, "The Body of Christ," Peter answers louder than anyone, "Amen Father!" He says it long-A Amen, not the broad restrained Anglican "ah-men," but hearty. And when I bring him the chalice, he takes a slurp, not a sip. I don't watch, but I imagine him licking his lips afterwards. He is unrestrained; he knows a good thing.

Yes, something else has its grip upon him. At Saint Thomas, we priests celebrate mass *ad orientem*, facing liturgical East, with our back to the people. I repeat the words of institution, elevate the host so that it can be seen, and from behind me comes an unmistakably clear, "Alleluia!" The people can't see it, but as I complete my genuflection, I smile.

It is a smile of thankful recognition. Peter in his desperately weakened state is giving voice to the real truth of what happens in the sacrament of the altar. Bread of the earth, a human product from native soil, is turned by God into the Body of his Son. The angels ever sing Alleluia for this gift of all gifts, and those who (like Peter) feel the heavenly grip cannot but join them.

Internet Reconnections

THE INTERNET HAS CHANGED about everything, it seems. It does get capitalized, "Internet," which strikes me as paradoxical, since it is the use of the Internet that has led to the loss of more capitals than all the earthquakes of history. One just doesn't capitalize letters in email addresses, or in the names of websites. If you do capitalize, you reveal yourself as a bit old fogeyish. So it's bn.com for the ubiquitous bookseller. On the other hand, we slip some unneeded capitals into SaintThomasChurch.org. We're old fogeyish enough to think they help the eyes, but you can "visit" us, as one says, without them.

It has changed social relationships profoundly. The first couple I married here had met on the Internet. He was in his late thirties and had posted information about himself on a dating website. A busy man making scads of money, he had forgotten about it and, he told me, he didn't even notice the monthly charge on his credit card bill. (I thought, that is a lot of money, not to take time to review your monthly charges.) But his personal information was also, perhaps, not that interesting. Until he heard from *her*, the first and I think only person to respond. They met, they came to like each other, they came to love each other, and now they wanted to be married. She had a grandparent who had been married at Saint Thomas, and so they had contacted us to see if they might be married here, even though they lived in California. Their initial contact with us was made, also, through the Internet.

This too strikes me as profoundly paradoxical, that social relationships could be created and fostered by a new thing that strips us of so many things that are personal. The telephone connected people by voice who, on account of distance, couldn't touch each other. (Advertising, of course, tries to promote the positive by appropriating the negative into a metaphor. If you are of an age you may remember the advertising campaign, years ago, to encourage the use of long distance telephoning. It was "Reach out and touch someone." The thing distance made impossible, touching, became a metaphor for speaking.) The Internet now connects people not only without physical presence, but without even voice or handwriting or the peculiarities of typewriter style. Everything is "virtual," all the physicality has been stripped away. And yet—the paradox—social connections happen.

Last year something happened for me that the Internet made possible. I had had a good friend in high school, the rare sort of friend with whom one spends hours talking every evening without tire. Even when we went to our different colleges, when we came back to our home town on holiday we would meet, go to an all-night truck-stop restaurant, and sit for even three hours drinking coffee. When I was about to graduate from St. John's College, I persuaded him to move out to Santa Fe with me and share an apartment. He did so, leaving behind his network of college friends in Norman, Oklahoma, and took up the life of a poor person in Santa Fe. And then my plans changed, and within the year I was married and I moved out. My friend I had left alone in an apartment far from the center of town. He was the best man at my wedding. But as a newly married fellow, I didn't see much of him. And in a few years I left town to go to seminary.

That was the last I saw of him. I had heard that he had gotten married himself to a young woman he met in the acting program at the College of Santa Fe, and that they had moved to Colorado. Occasionally I heard a tiny bit of news about him or his old Oklahoma family. But there had been no contact for decades, not since Santa Fe.

So it came into my mind one evening, about a year ago, that I might, as we have learned to say, "google" his name. His name came up. It was listed on a program for the production of a small theatre company in Colorado. I wrote to the company a brief explanation of who I was, and asked if they would forward my email to this person who had the same name as my friend from many years ago. In a few days I had a brief note from him, and then some longer letters. Last October Susan and I visited him and his wife and we had together a long, pleasant day of learning what had happened to each other over the past thirty years.

This story of mine is, it seems to me, not only about the Internet, although I find I cannot scorn an invention that has brought about the rediscovery of an old friend. It is a story of something theologians call "prevenient grace." Prevenient grace is God's way of giving us grace before we ask for it, God's way of going ahead of us into a situation and preparing things. For years I had the sense that I had not done my best by my friend, that I had caused him to move five hundred miles and then abandoned him in a strange town while I went on with my happy life. I had regret about that. And I was in a way thinking, as our meeting last October got closer, that one thing I wanted to do was to ask for his forgiveness. But when we met, when late into the day I started describing this as I have described it to you, he started laughing and interrupted me and corrected me. "Vic, it wasn't like that at all," he said. He knew before he moved to Santa Fe (something I had completely forgotten) that I might get married. There was no abandonment felt on his part, but instead a rich life that he looked back upon with humor and delight.

Will it be like that on Judgment Day, I wonder. At the end of all things, will capital-G God be like some sort of capital-I Internet, connecting us back to all the people we've had dealings with, connecting us back with all the things we have done? Some of those encounters, I know, we'd rather not have. But will it be that when we finally meet with the people we have not done right by, and we start to stammer out our regrets, that their eyes will sparkle, and clear laughter will fill the air? That they will say to us, "But it wasn't like that at all"? That we will discover that God has already changed everything into joy?

Being Unemployed

IT WAS MY FIRST EASTER as rector of the Church of the Resurrection in Hopewell Junction. The tradition of the parish, well-established by my predecessor and much to my liking, was to pull out all the stops for the Easter Vigil, which we celebrated in the middle of the night and followed by hearty breakfast in the undercroft. We had about eighty people at the Vigil that year, which was for us a very large congregation. As a result, not much work could go into the Easter morning Eucharist. About forty people came to that service, many of them first-timers. I told them all: Come back next week, there will be more people here! (And how many churches can say that they have more people on Low Sunday than on Easter Day?)

A young couple introduced themselves to me at the door, and they accepted my invitation, came the next week, and kept coming back. Their names were Deke and Debbie, and I came to learn that, as it happened, Deke had been a choir boy here at Saint Thomas. He was a bright fellow who worked in corporate communications. We enlisted him to design a logo for our parish and to re-design the Sunday leaflet. In fact, we enlisted him for a lot of things, as can happen in a small church (and can lead to "church burn-out"). Fortunately, Deke was also receiving from the church as well as giving to it, so that when he lost his job he had a spiritual base to fall back on.

He had six months of unemployment benefits, money he and his wife needed to make their house payments. Her salary alone would not have been adequate. He worked hard throughout those six months to find another job, and nothing happened. I remember the combination of anxiety and faith that he had. He wasn't giving up, but he didn't know what he would do.

Finally, on the last day of the last week, he got word that he would be hired in communications for a corporation in Connecticut. He would not have to move, they would not have to give up their house, their financial needs would be met (in fact, more than met). I remember him giving thanks to God for his new job. I also remember the next thing he said to God: "Couldn't you have told me earlier?"

Faith is like that: it comes to us in the waiting. If God had told Deke that at the end of the twenty-six weeks he would get a job, and it would be a good job, then Deke would not have needed to exercise his faith. I learned a lot from Deke in this. And yet it still seems to me a very difficult thing. I often want to say to God, for myself or for someone else who is going through a hard time: *Couldn't you tell us how this will turn out?*

Other people's faith has been harmed, not helped, in unemployment. There was a woman who worked hard to get new professional credentials, taking night classes and so forth. She told me she didn't have time for church, between work and study and family. And I could see she was very busy. When she finally graduated and got her new and good job, she didn't return to church to give thanks. She had left church in the hard times, and didn't return in the good.

Some of you reading this may be going through hard times, and what I want to say to you is: don't give up on church when it's hard. It is important in hard times to keep talking with God. Ask him questions like, Why is this happening? Can you tell me how this will turn out? Ask him whatever questions you have. And come to church for the spiritual food that God gives us to be nourishment for our souls, when we are employed and when we aren't.

Recently a gentleman told me how it was that he started coming to Saint Thomas. It was several decades ago. He was a student, and had to get from Union Square to the upper east side—a distance of two or three miles. He had enough money for the bus, but that was all the money he had. And so he walked. As he passed by, something about Saint Thomas grabbed his attention, and he came in to pray. He didn't know what to do, he needed help, and he prayed to God. As he rose from his prayers he saw on the floor by the kneeler a ten-dollar bill. "What do I do with this?" He considered the alternatives, and in the end decided it was God's gift to him, grocery money, in those days, for a week and a half.

Make of it what you will. He keeps coming to church, even though his life has been rough. Lots of us keep coming. God seems to provide what we need in the end, even if the way there is not easy; and even if our vision is not clear, in the end God seems to provide.

Is It Expensive?

F ATHER, WE COULD HAVE filled the church all over again with the people we turned away tonight." That was the usher speaking to the rector at about 12:45 AM early on December 25. There are seriously big crowds at Saint Thomas in December, a tide of humanity coming to church and culminating with the Christmas Eve midnight mass at which, as the usher said, we have to turn away several hundred people. There simply isn't a single seat left. Christmas morning also lures in a crowd, this year nearly eleven hundred people, for a service perhaps even more beautiful than the midnight one because less frantic. When it's all over, we clergy stand at the doors and shake hands, greeting friends and strangers with "Merry Christmas" and "Peace" and even "Good morning!" (particularly effective at 12:45 AM).

When the crowds had thinned out on Christmas Day, a man came to me holding his Christmas program. He had it open to the notice of next Sunday's services. "Can anyone come?" he said. I mistook his question for one about participation in the sacrament, and so I was telling him everyone is welcome but only those who are baptized should receive communion. "Are you baptized?" I asked. He wasn't, but he also wasn't asking about communion. He was just asking about coming. He pointed into the church, his gesture taking in all at once the high stone walls, the reredos, the stained glass.

"Can anyone come?" he repeated. "You don't have to be rich?"

Saint Thomas obviously looks like a rich person's place. I looked at him. "You don't have to be rich," I said. "Anyone can come."

"But," he asked, "is it expensive?" I finally figured out the point of his questions. He thought there was an admissions charge for church services.

"No," I said, "it's free." And with a smile I said, "It's very expensive. But it's free."

What sped through my mind at that moment was the thought of the millions of dollars we need to raise for capital projects. The stained glass needs repair; some of it is buckling dangerously; that project is some $20 million. Our organ needs replacing; that's another seven to nine million. Not to mention that our annual operating deficit, the excessive draw-down from our invested funds, is itself a million or two. And I thought at the very same time about the question mark that the current financial crisis has hung over those projects.

It's very expensive: Saint Thomas's mere physical presence entails a critically large quantity of money. But, nonetheless, it is free. And it is a great gift to the city, to have this place of wonder where anyone can come and be overwhelmed with the beauty of God.

This inquisitive and unbaptized man was looking for he knew not what, and he was concerned lest he not be able to pay the cost. So, despite my inability at the time to explain it all to him, I wanted him to have the truth. And I think that the words I spontaneously said to him were, by God's grace, true words, true as far down as you care to go. For it is the case that Christianity is both expensive and yet free. What does God want from us? On the one hand, nothing; he is our maker, our redeemer, our beginning and our end. There is nothing we can give to God: everything is sheer gift, gift from him to us. So it's all free. And yet, as T. S. Eliot would remind us to add: "costing not less than everything." God needs nothing from us, and yet he wants something that is more expensive than any financial or material sacrifice we could give him. He wants our hearts. God is calling us to love him, to love him totally, to gaze upon the newborn babe with the rapture that seizes its own heart and says, "Here, take this; I give it to you."

You can come back here as often as you want; it's absolutely free. But watch out: God wants from you the most expensive thing of all. Just as he gave himself to us in the child Jesus, so he wants you to give yourself to him in love.

Busyness

T HE BLACKBERRY, THE IPOD, the Palm Pilot, the Bluetooth ear
thing, wireless Internet access, the laptop computer, and (going
back) the cell phone, the car phone, the Dictaphone; silicone chips,
transistors, portable DVD players, portable radios: in entertainment, in
work, at home and on the road, human life seems to have been moving
and still to be moving in one direction only, the direction of accelera-
tion. Our lives get only faster. There is ever more to do: more music to
download, more emails, more messages, more tasks, more connections.
It is exciting, to be on this dizzying romp with post-industrial society.

All the products that make possible our ever-connected life, the
Blackberries and Blueteeth and cells and pods, they are monuments of
human achievement. Many of them have already been acquisitioned,
as we now say, by the custodial institutions of human greatness. The
plastic transistor radio and the smooth buttonless iPhone are as much
museum objects as the Penny Black postage stamp, the Louis XIV
bureau brisé, and the antique marble god.

These products that make our lives run faster, they have done
much good for us. Thanks to the Internet, the personal digital assistant, and the home computer, it is possible for work schedules to be
pliant to an unprecedented degree. Among other benefits, certain

types of workers can also now be home caregivers, on flexible schedules. A doctor can take in a school play or go to the gym and still be available in need. Consider how the cassette tape player, although now thoroughly passé, made it possible for people to turn driving time into a time of self-education. In a thousand ways, in perhaps a thousand times a thousand ways, human beings are more productive now than they've ever been before. And our race is only getting faster.

I want to emphasize that I think this is a good thing. But good or bad, one must recognize that accelerating technological change is an unavoidable feature of our life. And as every one of us knows, there is a price to pay. Our nonstop busyness is the cause of an inchoate anxiety. We fear that we are so busy that we are losing something of great value, perhaps without even noticing that it's going away.

What is it that we fear we are losing? It can't be an older style of life that was experienced more leisurely, for such a life exists only in false nostalgia—there never was (for most people) a quiet, leisured life. The farmers on the prairie worked 24/7 even more than the most harried post-industrial, Blackberry-leashed professional. Those farmers labored against recalcitrant nature and unpredictable weather, making clothes, canning vegetables, repairing roofs and fences, improvising tools, husbanding their animals, without vacation, without rest, sunrise to sunset and, in the home, by oil lamp into the evening. It is not leisure that we fear losing, for our race has always had to work, at least since the time that the Garden of Eden was closed to us.

When I was a year or so out of college, while visiting the home of my former tutor Michael Ossorgin, I was asked if I was still playing the piano. I regretted that I wasn't; "I've been too busy," I said. Mr. Ossorgin—although an Orthodox priest, his honorific according to custom at St. John's College was "Mr."—chided me to keep with the piano, but his wife tried to rise in my defense. "He says he's too busy," she said; whereupon in his thick Russian accent he said, "If he's busy, he should be busy with *it*" (meaning the piano).

We can't get away from being busy, we humans, but I think our fear is that we aren't being busy with the right things. These things that accelerate our lives and make us exponentially more productive, we fear that they also may be diverting our attention. Our lives are spinning and they spin ever faster. But spinning is characteristic of the world: the earth spins on an axis; the solar system circles around the sun; even galaxies spin and turn. We can't but spin, but the good news is that there is always a center to our spinning. And that center is still. Think of a well-trained ballet dancer executing consecutive, non-stop pirouettes: it is breathtaking, and it is possible only because he stands still at the center of all his movement.

What is the stillness at the center of human life? Behind the Blackberry, the Palm Pilot, the Bluetooth, and the iPhone, what is "the still point of the turning world"? T. S. Eliot took us there: "neither flesh nor fleshless, neither from nor towards," the still point is a place of paradox, the location of the dance, which is not fixity or absence of motion. It is, of course, a way of thinking about God. God is the still point, the source of all the busyness of our lives, the center of our work and the center of our play, the center and cause, in fact, of the entire human dance. The danger of busyness is that we forget the still point around which our lives spin.

We can't escape busyness; it is our lot and nature as humans. But we can, I think, cultivate strategies of recollection, moments when we "spot" ourselves on that one enduring reality at the center of our lives. That is why we pray; that is, perhaps, why you have at some time gone to church: to retreat briefly from the spinning world in order to apprehend the point of it all.

Still Busy

THE NIGHT BEFORE HE DIED, our Lord took with his intimate friends his final meal, which included (we presume among other foods) the deeply symbolic bread and wine. He took the bread, and after he had given thanks for it to his Father, he broke it. When he then allotted the bread to his friends, he did so with the instruction that they were to receive this bread and to eat it, and furthermore, they were to continue to do so "in remembrance of me." Likewise, he took the cup of wine, and once he had thanked his Father for it, he passed the cup around all his friends, insisting that they drink of it, now, and that they continue to do so, so that he would be remembered.

The liturgical theologian Dom Gregory Dix has called this the most obeyed command in history. What Jesus told his friends to do has been done, day after day, week after week, year after year, century upon century, not only in the land that was Jesus' home, but in every piece of this earth, in every language spoken of men. There is probably no hour of the day, no *minute* of the day, no minute of *any* day, on which there aren't people somewhere, gathered to remember Jesus by speaking these eucharistic words over bread and wine.

What I want to suggest is that the Eucharist shows us what it means to be the center of the world—in the words of Eliot, "the still point of the turning world." The altar is a point of stillness. You can come there, and I encourage you to think of coming there, as a short retreat from the ceaseless and accelerating spinning of the world, and there you can find calm, even as the world spins around. There you can find meaning, even if the world races thoughtlessly by. There you can find love that is unchanging, ceaselessly offering itself, the free gift of God's life-blood for the world.

I like to think of coming to the Eucharist not as a stepping out of time but rather a stepping further into time, stepping as it were into the center of time. You might think that Christian worship is an escape from the world. But in truth it is not so: to approach the altar is not to leave the world behind but to move into its heart. We do not step out of time but down into its heart, not away from the spinning and clueless world but further into the world, to its unspinning and meaningful core.

One Saturday I came to Saint Thomas to celebrate the 12:10 mass. James, an acolyte, had come to assist me. When we came out to begin, there was no congregation. Still we went ahead with the mass, did the readings, said the prayers, prepared the altar, consecrated the Bread and the Wine, and received Communion. As I said the prayers, I realized that James and I were participating in that which is hidden from the world and yet supports the whole world. The God we touch here is the true God, who holds the cosmos in being, unceasingly and unchangingly. It doesn't take a crowd of people for this to be true. Two thousand, two hundred, twenty, or just two: it's still the heart of the world.

Mr. Ossorgin told me that if I was going to be busy, I should be busy with my piano. That was particular advice. Let me give general advice. If we are going to be busy, we should be busy with the Eucharist.

As he was telling me that the piano should have a place in my busy life, so Jesus tells all of us that this Eucharist should have a place in our busy lives. In fact, it already has a place. It's the center.

Come often to touch the center, the still point of the turning world.

From Choir School to Church

ALMOST EVERY DAY WE WALK from the choir school to the church. The boys will do it four or five times a week; I may do it twice a day. We're not unusual; as I've said before, all New Yorkers walk a lot—it probably makes New York one of the healthiest places to live in the country. The walk from choir school to church is two long blocks and five short blocks, or a bit more than half a mile. There are a dozen different ways you can make the walk, including several routes that take you *through* buildings. (I felt uncomfortable about that when some eighth graders first showed it to me. But then Philip, an architect who knows the regulations that govern construction, explained that these buildings were allowed to go higher than would otherwise have been legal *precisely because* they granted public access from one street to the other.) And along all those different ways, people start to know you by face. They might nod or speak, but even if they keep a determinedly stern countenance, you know they know you.

Since clergy at Saint Thomas are expected to dress in clericals (black clergy shirt with suit), these people know me as a priest. Peter, a regular panhandler at the first corner, smiles and says, "Have a good day, Father." I greet him by name and return the smile. The barbers will nod in greeting, if they're out on the sidewalk. Even the people with whom you've never talked turn out to recognize you. I once went in casual clothes to buy an umbrella. "Father," the man in the store said to me, "you are a priest, right?" He wanted to know about that woman he often saw on my arm. I explained that she was my wife, that I was a priest in the Episcopal Church, that we can marry.

A concierge once stopped me as I passed his revolving doors. "Father, can I talk to you?" I try not to encourage this sort of thing: when I'm walking, I want to get where I'm going. But it became clear right away that this fellow wasn't out for money, so I stopped and gave him a lot of my time. Maybe two minutes. He explained a moral dilemma that he was in, concerned with some carpentry work done on the side for a tenant who now wasn't paying him. On the street, you don't take long to get to the guts of things. It strikes me that it's like emergency room work for a theologian. I told him he should not feel guilty, ever, about seeking justice; that justice needs to be fair to everybody, thus fair both to him and to the man for whom he did the work. And I found myself saying something I had never before said while standing on a sidewalk: "May I pray for you?" I said a short and direct prayer, and blessed him with a discreet sign of the cross.

I saw him again several times, and he gave me brief updates. Now I think he must have moved on, because he hasn't been there for awhile.

Just above I made a comparison with emergency room work. There was a parishioner several years ago who explained that the emergency room was his preferred sort of medical practice. Other doctors get to know their patients and stay with them, share their lives, for years; or at least, that's an ideal (perhaps more antique than real). But, he explained, those other doctors never get the satisfaction of quickly fixing a specific situation. "In the ER," he said, "I order the tests I need, and I get the results, and *we solve the problem*." Of course, no problem is finally solved—every emergency room will tell you to follow up with your regular physician—but there is a distinct satisfaction that the ER doctor enjoys. Sometimes, even on the street, even when I'm trying to ignore all the people around me, this theologian has discovered such satisfaction. The city seems infinitely complicated. There are millions of stories here, millions of problems. One day you're just walking along, and you get to speak a few words of truth, and it's like light coming into a dark room.

I hope he followed up with his regular Physician.

Conversation in the Dairy Aisle

You SHOULD GET whole milk; it's good for satiety." She pronounced it suh-TIE-eh-tee. I was holding the economical house brand no-fat yoghurt. It was 9:45 in the evening, and Whole Foods was going to close in fifteen minutes. I looked over at the short, thin, black-haired woman. Those were the first words she said to me.

I like to think I've become a New Yorker—that a complete stranger's suddenly telling me which yoghurt I ought to buy, and why, is nothing to pull me off my stride. And to be sure, it didn't strike me as absurd or ridiculous. Yet it did slow me down. I thought, *Where I come from, we say hello before we give advice.*

I nodded and mumbled a smile. She didn't smile. She pointed to the container in her hands: Stonyfield Farm Whole Milk Yoghurt. "You need to eat fat," the short skinny woman said to the tall skinny man. "If you don't get the fat you need, you'll graze all morning. You know, *graze*, eating junk all day that you don't need and that's bad for you."

This is why Father Stafford thinks I'm a wimp. I just stand here and don't tell her to buzz off.

"You should eat without having the television on or music playing or reading a book. That's the problem. People aren't paying attention while they eat." I think: *When do they read the newspaper?* But I say nothing, just try to look benign. She darted over to her cart, then darted back. "Look, this one's organic. The one you've got, no good. This one has living L. Acidophilus cultures. It's good for your intestines."

Now we're getting personal. What does she know about my intestines?

She departed as abruptly as she had appeared, no farewell, no question, just—gone. I pondered the low-price low-fat yoghurt in my hand. Then the corner of a thought that I hadn't had for ten years caught in my mind. I put back the store brand, and loaded into my basket a quart of Stonyfield. Organic. Whole milk.

…It was Stonyfield yoghurt, I remembered, that Elizabeth used to bring over to Susan, back in my old parish in Dutchess County, in the years after Susan's brain tumor was found and as she went through the year of chemotherapy and the adjustments that came after. Elizabeth was artsy, a bright intellectual with crafting instincts, with a carpenter-husband, and with two babies in her future. She would come over and see Susan and bring yoghurt and fruit and sweet cheer and happy talk. Sometimes they'd sit outside and have a picnic. They'd talk about children's books and writing, and I think they read to each other.

Yes, it was that distinctive brown Stonyfield container that Elizabeth brought….

So here I am, out at 10 PM on the coldest day yet here in New York, savoring the intemperate intrusion of the intense woman in the dairy aisle. Did she bear for me a message tinged with the divine? I wonder if, perhaps, I wasn't brusque with her because she had something I needed to hear—not about acidophilus, but about *philos* in another sense: the old friends, happier days, perhaps; the longing that we must never lose, and which leads us home to God? Elizabeth—and Susan—used to call it Sweet Desire.

Did Jesus Die for Them All?

I N THE MIDST OF OUR Holy Week services a few years ago—what some of us call "all church, all the time," and which are resplendent with music and ceremony—Max, our parish verger, turned to me. "Father Theologian, do you think our Lord had all this in mind when he was dying on the cross?"

It is an interesting question at any time, what Jesus had in mind. Herbert McCabe has taught us to approach the question in terms of what we can say of Jesus. Since Jesus is at once fully God and fully human, we can say of Jesus anything that we would say of God *and* anything we would say of a first-century Palestinian man. *As God*, Jesus knows everything, for God, who unchangingly holds all things in being, cannot be ignorant of anything in the universe, past, present, or future. He knows everything actively, which means that all events are somehow "present" to him at once. But *as man*, Jesus is immersed in the patterns of time. He knows, as man, the future only as something not yet formed, a realm of freedom, possibility, and chance. Thus *as God* Jesus on the cross knows the fantastically beautiful services offered at Saint Thomas Church, including services which focus upon the very death that he is undergoing. Yet *as man* Jesus knows none of this.

(Of course, we cannot comprehend how both these things can be true concerning the single person, Jesus; but is that an insurmountable problem? We also cannot comprehend how a common electron can be both a particle and a wave, or how a negative number can have a square root.)

When we consider the death of Christ our minds are swept over by the breadth of God's saving plan. Experienced, say, at the Church of the Resurrection in Hopewell Junction, at midnight with a hundred people holding candles and singing "Christ is risen from the dead Trampling down death by death," Easter is believable: by dying, he conquered death for us, for those buried in this cemetery, and for all those other people we don't know and we can't see.

Now follow me to Fifth Avenue on Easter morning. The line for the eleven o'clock service started forming before the eight o'clock was finished. By ten o'clock or so, all the good central nave seats will be filled. By eleven o'clock, every seat in every alcove or corner, and every balcony seat, will have been taken, and there will be folks standing in the Narthex watching through the glass. They will keep coming, and some going, throughout the next hour and a half; indeed, to look at the church in its Easter glory, they will come throughout the day and even the coming week. We are talking serious crowds here, people that none of us will ever know (at least in this life). They are looking. Some are kneeling, a few quietly weep; others are curious and sometimes rude— but you wonder, even in the "touristy" cases, what might be going on in their soul. What is the story of their life? How did they get here? Do they know what they are seeking? What is God doing for them?

Let me put it this way. For those of us in the church week upon week, both laity and clergy, we can come to think of ourselves as a minority and perhaps elite group that has recognized something of beauty that should not be lost, and as a consequence we organize our lives to carry it to the next generation. That is, we may think of church as a significant cultural repository, along the lines of the museum, the opera, the symphony, the parks conservancy. And it is true, deeply true, that the church has something of great importance to transmit from generation to generation. *But it is not in any sense an elite business.* It is our challenge to apprehend the unbounded range of God's intention to save the world. Jesus' death and resurrection—as the slang phrase has it—was not only for those of us who *get it*.

Wisdom

FOR DECADES I BRISTLED whenever I heard, "When you get older, you'll understand." That's such a cop-out, I'd say. "You aren't going to make an argument, you aren't going to give reasons, you're just going to assert that you know better because you're older?" I'd throw some Eliot back at them. "Do not let me hear of the wisdom of old men, but of their fear"! Time and age and experience don't add up to wisdom; they could just as well add up to cynicism, indifference, or plain laziness.

There were other things that bothered me, like referring to young people as "the church of the future." What do you mean, "the church of the future"? Are the only real members of the church the grown-ups? Don't we baptize babies? Aren't the young people part of *the church of today*?...And then the young adults, the new professionals, the new parents: they too are the church of the future? What are the implicit standards in such a statement? That the "real" Christian, the "fulfilled" Christian, is a successful businessperson who has done well and is now able to retire?

But then something happened to me. With a class of undergraduates a few years ago I re-read the *Nicomachean Ethics*. In that book Aristotle explains that ethics is a difficult subject. In fact, he says, it shouldn't be taught to anyone who is under, say, forty years old. Younger people need training and apprenticeship and experience. And only those who get good training are capable of going on to the study of higher things.

And there I was, on the upper side of forty, with a room full of twenty-somethings, reading a book that claimed they shouldn't be reading it. What would I say to them? Well, I didn't actually say it, but the thought was certainly present in my mind. *When you get older…*

In the academic world there is a venerable custom of presenting a good teacher, who is approaching retirement, a collection of papers written in his honor by his onetime students and colleagues. In some cases, the papers will be given to him publicly, and he can respond to them. When the exercise is seriously undertaken, the "festschrift" digs into the history of the teacher's scholarship. There will be references to his early work in the philosophy of religion (say), and how that gave way to questions in fundamental theology. Someone will talk about the friendships he, a Roman Catholic, developed with evangelical protestants, and the challenges that arose from his scholarship in ecumenism. And at the end, the scholar rises to speak.

I was at such a colloquium for Bill Shea, held at the 2008 conference of the College Theology Society. It is easy (and easier for me now in my fifties than it was in my twenties) to grow sentimental at such a moment. Professor Shea was about to retire; the festschrift in his honor was about to be published; we could see in him what it meant to give your life as a theologian. Even so, he managed to save the moment from pure sentimentality. "I *know* God exists," he asserted clearly; "I *believe* Jesus rose from the dead." The distinction of knowledge and belief is fundamental. We can know the existence of God—reason makes it clear from the very existence of things; God is the unknown reason for everything that exists for as long as it exists. But we can only believe in Jesus' resurrection. Bill Shea was being clear that he had staked his life on the resurrection; yet, nonetheless, he could not say that he knew it to be true.

Then he said something else, something that gave evidence of an understanding that goes beyond the mastery of argument. "I know God exists," he said, "but sometimes I wonder, is he out to lunch?" It was a playful formulation—God, of course, no more needs lunch than he needs burnt offerings—but Shea was deadly serious. The recent natural disasters, hurricane and tsunami and earthquake; the human disasters of intertribal massacre; where is God in all this? At the end of the day, it is quite true, there is no accounting for evil. The argument is strong and convincing, at least to me, that the fact of evil does not argue against God's existence, nor against the goodness of God. But it is a truth we cannot get our minds around. The elder theologian, upheld by the praise and love of his colleagues and students, author of a dozen books, leading member of a learned society, shows his wisdom by the question he puts at the end. "What I want to know—Is God out to lunch?"

Another question for an honest prayer.

Do You Still Have a Job?

I WAS GETTING MY HAIR CUT by someone I'd seen a few times before. Once she was underway with the snip-snip action, she said to me: "Do you still have a job?"

I don't think she knows yet that I'm a priest—I tend to have my hair cut on my day off when I'm in civvies, and I can't recall her asking me before what I did for a living. But now she's, as they say, "feeling a bit of hurt," because fewer people are coming in, or they're coming in less frequently. "Women who used to have their hair washed and set every week, now they're every other week. Lots of people tell me they've lost their job. It's slowing down here."

Everyone I know who still has a job knows lots of people who don't. "The being-laid-off process is brutal," one guy was explaining to me. "They set it up so you don't know it's coming. You're called into your manager's office and told, in a very few words, that your position has been eliminated and that you no longer have a job. It's all carefully planned. They won't let you go back to your office. One fellow I know, he asked if he could just go get his family pictures. 'We'll mail them to you,' was the response. You turn over your ID, your building pass, and an escort takes you out of the building. No good-byes, no wrapping up projects, no chance even to shut down the computer and turn out the lights. You are just gone."

Of course, it's not that brutal everywhere, but it is harsh on the spirit, however it happens. One day you have projects, colleagues, a boss, tasks, goals, everything that being at work can give you. The next day you are unemployed. What will you do?

It is beyond my capacity to give employment advice, except to offer prayer and encouragement to persist with hope. Once back in college, when I was faced with a difficult problem, I asked my tutor, Michael Ossorgin, for advice. He told me to take my problem to God. "Lay it on the altar," he said, "and then work like hell." It's the only time I remember him (a Russian and a priest) saying "hell" in that manner. But it is good advice that captures the paradox of complete trust in God combined with full human responsibility. We should turn over to God all our problems, like everything in life whether it is a problem or not. "Take it to the Lord in prayer," as the old song has it. But at the same time, we should apply ourselves one hundred percent to solving our problem. Turning something over to God does not mean it ceases to be something we work on.

So that's what I tell people who have lost their jobs: place your situation in God's hands, while working full-time on finding your next position. But as I kept thinking about my hair cutter, it seemed to me that there was another way to consider her question.

It comes to everyone, some day or another, to lose their job and never get another. If you do not die on the job, one of two things will happen: either you will retire, or you will be laid off and never work again. So in the end, everyone answers negatively. "No, I don't have a job anymore," we will all have to say.

But will we be truly jobless?

Go with me to the hospital to visit Edna. You know Edna as a strong woman who raised two children alone after her husband's early death and has somehow kept her life together with a variety of cleaning jobs, both as an employee and as self-employed. Now sixty, she has had a stroke, and you fear that, with her justifiable pride in her self-sufficiency, she will not adjust to being unable to work. You sit with her for maybe ten minutes, small talk carried on patiently if slowly, and then with her good hand she squeezes yours. She tells you she has an important job to do in the hospital. "Yes?" you say to her, "a job?" She tells you her job: she's praying for you and for everyone in the church.

Do you still have a job? There is always this: a whole world needing to be prayed for.

Waiting Room

A DOCTOR WAS LEADING a seminar on the Hippocratic Oath. Around the table were about twenty-five of us, some doctors, some married to doctors, but more of us from non-medical professions. Our seminar leader pointed out that for most of the history of medicine, the physicians who took that oath had very little they could do for their patients: perhaps some pain control, some received lore about herbal medicine, and of course the ability to accompany a patient in his illness and to keep confidence. How different medicine is today.

Doctors and patients alike decry the down-sides of the specialization of contemporary medicine. If one of us has, say, a brain tumor, we end up in the hands of many physicians: the neurologist, the neurosurgeon, the radiologist, the oncologist, and so on. This is on top of our regular doctor and, for half our species, a gynecologist. To have all these doctors is a luxury in a sense, made possible in western societies by the immense amount of money we devote to medicine, through various combinations of insurance payments and governmental appropriations. To have all these doctors is also a blessing, because any one of them has almost godlike knowledge of his specialty, which knowledge can benefit us in ways unimaginable even as recently as the time of our childhood. Doctors today have so much knowledge that it seems they can cure, or are likely to cure, most of the things that afflict the children of men. If only we can find the right doctor, get in to see the right specialist, then all shall be well.

But this luxury and blessing comes at a cost. For one thing, it is hard to keep the patient together, to see the good of the whole person, when he has so many specialists looking after him. For another, the patient spends a lot of time going from doctor to doctor.

You make your appointment. Being conscientious, you arrive early: it's a new doctor, you didn't want to be late, you didn't know how long it would take you to get there. You are twenty minutes early. The waiting room is nearly full. There is some talking. There is a television in the corner. You try to read the book you brought with you. About forty-five minutes pass—the doctor is running late—and then your name is called. She takes time with you, and you like that, telling her as best you can what your symptoms are. She examines you attentively, and then orders two tests for you to have done—you'll have to go to another office for the tests—and states that she'd like you to come back in six weeks.

So you've taken out altogether, with travel and waiting time, maybe three hours of your day, for the sake of those ten or fifteen minutes. You like her, and you don't begrudge her the time. But it is real time—real cost. Now you're going to do the same again: phone for an appointment, visit a different office, have some tests done. Then you'll phone her office, try to make sure the test results have been transmitted and not lost, make your appointment, and appear for your return visit.

And you will do this, not only for your present condition, but time upon time upon time for the rest of your life. Mammograms, colonoscopies, blood tests, broken bones, joints that wear down, lungs that fill up, blood vessels that are too tight, the heart itself, the nervous system; not to mention the things that come at you from outside: flu, other viruses, skin disease, infections of new sorts. You are sitting in one of those waiting rooms, children on the floor, television in the corner, book on your lap, but you aren't reading your book or watching TV or listening to the talk around you. You are thinking, *I'm going to be in rooms like this for as long as I live.* I'm glad to be called out of this room, to see the doctor, to have the hope that my condition can be better understood and perhaps cured. But whether for the thing that brought me here today or for something else, most assuredly I will be back in this room or another like it, waiting again.

A lot of our life is waiting. There are spiritual disciplines that we might develop. A simple one is to pray for people who are in the waiting room with you. Another is gratitude. What here can I be thankful for, while I am waiting? Sometimes I notice there is no TV and no background music in the waiting room—believe me, I give thanks for that. And all of us who have the luxury of access to doctors should be thankful.

Perhaps it's too obvious to mention, but I think the waiting room is a parable for our lives as a whole. Something is not right with us. We suffer the infections of sin, and we face the certainty of our mortality. We are waiting to see the physician of our souls. It's not a perfect parable—this life has eternal significance in terms of history and decision, things we do, characters we make of ourselves. This life is not simply waiting. Nonetheless there is truth in the parable of the waiting room. Someday our name will be called. We will leave this waiting room and meet our true Physician face to face.

Ever Connected

BACK IN THE 1980S, when I first lived in New York, there were people on the street who were talking to themselves. When you passed them on the sidewalk, you looked the other way.

Now it seems everyone is talking to herself. Or himself.

You pause at a corner to wait for traffic. In front of you, a smartly dressed young woman is describing her date from last night. You want to know simultaneously both more and less than she's saying. The light changes. A compact young man in a suit is saying something about prices. Another is saying angry words that you can't make out. On your right you hear half of a conversation in Spanish. You are surrounded by people who are talking, but they do not talk to each other.

When cell phones were just beginning to be ubiquitous, a *New York Times* columnist observed a man, on a crowded bus, talking loudly into his cell phone. He was boasting of his job and some recent accomplishment. In the middle of his talk, his phone rang. Visibly embarrassed and briefly shaken, he looked around, then pushed a button to take the call.

My rector says that New York is a city of actors.

I have resisted devices with earpieces—from the Walkman to the iPod. Even the earpiece that attaches to my Palm Treo, which could turn it into a device for listening to books on tape (sorry, make that "audio books"), I say no thanks, I'd rather not. I like to walk with all my senses engaged, to carry on a silent dialogue with myself about these blocks I know so well and which yet surprise me almost every day. I notice the progress in the renovations of the buildings I pass, the new skyscraper going up on 57th, the sudden appearance of a sidewalk shed or its just as sudden disappearance. I turn on Sixth in the evening after a class, and there is the famous corner chef, with his aluminum cart and thirty or fifty people waiting in line. Where does he come from? How do they know about him? I walk past and scan the billboards at City Center and Carnegie. It's too late now, but earlier in the day I would have seen my friend the fruit seller who nods kindly in my direction, although I think he is uncertain what to make of my collar. If it's Easter, Petrossian will have its Easter breads in the window, and its miniature Pascha.

And I might pray. Dean James Fenhagen told us when we were seminary students that we could pray while we rode the subway. It's always possible to pray, to give thanks for a bit of beauty or delight, or to intercede briefly for someone you see. And I guess today we don't need to worry about praying out loud. People will just think we're connected to our cell phone.

Confession

DONALD CAMPBELL WAS RECTOR of Holy Faith in Santa Fe back in the 1970s. His ministry, and the experience of life in that parish, were the occasions God used to draw me into the priesthood. "It's the best job in the world," he said. "People let you into the heart of their lives, births, death, joy, tragedy. A priest is welcome. You can just walk in." We learned that he practiced what he preached. Susan had gone into the hospital briefly (false labor), and a day or two later, unannounced, he was knocking at the door of our low-rent adobe apartment. Only a brief visit, a self-deprecating remark, a prayer, and he was gone. He was welcome.

Times are different now, and New Yorkers are more different still. Privacy and security are valued, and no one this side of law enforcement visits unannounced. Nonetheless, priests do find that they are given access to the insides of life. People make appointments to talk. They want to see you. Now a persistent question in my life has been, how do truths of theology make a difference on the ground? Is theology just talk, or is it real? So to be a priest, to enter the insides of life, is in a way an opportunity to pose a question to God. What difference do you, God, make to this person's situation?

At Saint Thomas there is a regular announcement that clergy are available to hear confessions by appointment. Sermons are sometimes given on the subject, and "sacramental confession" is the announced title of a session of the rector's Christian doctrine class each year. I assist our rector, Father Mead, in that class, and one year he began the session by asking, "Father Austin, what do you think when a person comes to make a confession with you?" I don't know what I said—I think many different things—but I know what he said. It is a beautiful thing, he said, that God has brought this person to want to make a confession. And it is a privilege to be able to hear their confession as a priest.

It goes without saying that confession is confidential. I remind penitents who come to me that not only am I not to speak to another person of what they say, I will not even bring it up with them without their initiating it. God has, in fact, given me something like an "erase button" in my mind, which can make for awkwardness when a person does in fact want to make reference to their confession and I have to ask them to tell me again what it was we talked about. This business of confidentiality means, too, that I cannot speak even in a vague way about who sees me for confession or what topics they bring up.

But I do from time to time make my own confession. And what I find to be true in myself is what I see in others: that God is at work in our lives in quiet ways and often hidden dimensions that we do not see. It is by confessing our sins that we come to be aware of the working of God's grace. God is at work in our lives already—but how much better it is, how much more encouraging it is, when we can be shown something of what it is that he is up to. That awareness comes about in confession.

It is a paradox. By owning up to our short-fallings, back-steppings, wanderings, cruelties—the things that are so much a part of us, but we hide from view—we can discover how much good is happening already in our lives. And we discover that the good that is happening is God's work.

G. K. Chesterton's fictional detective, Father Brown, was able to solve mysteries of crime because he had the experience of hearing confessions. But more than that: he was able to be a good hearer of confessions because he understood the criminal heart. And he understood that heart because he understood his own. A real priest knows that every sin, whatever it might be, is something of which his heart is capable. I've never heard a sin that I cannot imagine myself doing. But the very articulation of a sin, the asking for forgiveness and for help—that is already something God is doing. Even if the sin we are confessing seems hopeless to us, simply the fact that we are sorrowful about it is a sign that God is at work. And if he is at work, things are far from hopeless.

Father Campbell was right. It is the most wonderful thing in the world, to be privileged to look on the insides and discover that everything theology tells us about God is true. God acts preveniently, giving us good things even before we ask. Through Christ sins are really taken away. And we are being transformed into his likeness, with a glorious destiny the groundwork for which is even now being laid.

Let Down?

S HE HAD PREPARED FOR MONTHS for her confirmation, and that
was just counting her time here at Saint Thomas. About a decade
earlier, in her home country, she was about to be confirmed when a
radical Muslim uprising made it dangerous. "To get confirmed was
like drawing a bull's-eye, saying 'Shoot Me.'" So now, at last, the sacrament was to be hers.

She expected to feel the Holy Spirit come upon her. In her country, she told me, some people are overtaken by tongues or ecstasy when
the bishop's hands are laid upon them. After the service, at coffee hour,
she told me nothing happened; she hadn't felt anything. I was trying
to introduce her around—I knew she had no family present—but
what could I say? "Sometimes we feel things," I said, "and sometimes
we don't; but our feelings don't change the reality." She didn't look
persuaded.

I thought back to another confirmation, many years ago. The
confirmand was a professional woman who had been brought back
to the church, in part through my teaching and encouragement. She
was a great blessing to our little parish: so much energy, so much wit
and excitement over true doctrine and service to one another. Finally
her day came also, the glorious day of confirmation. It was followed, I

gathered, by one of the worst weeks of her life. Doubts, harshness of character, and other old things that she thought were long past came back upon her with ferocity. She asked: why is this happening to me, now, in the week right after I received the grace of confirmation?

It happens often, this apparent let-down after a significant event of grace. You might feel it the week after Easter, wondering what happened to all the beautiful flowers, the great music, the crowds shouting Alleluia. Was it real? Or were we merely deceived?

Back in my seminary days, I returned for my second year of study and found that two of our faculty members had separated from their spouses over the summer. This on top of fellow students who were divorcing felt to me like a terrible sadness. "Of all places," I said to Rusty, my spiritual director, "of all places, why is divorce happening here in the seminary?" He looked me squarely in the face. "Victor," he said, "if you were the Devil, where would you focus your energies?"

Yikes! "You believe the Devil is real?" was my comment to him. It is serious business, this which we are engaged in. Church is not just a game. O the temptations, for those who get close to the church, the temptations are to think that all this is just mechanics, mere words, a simple matter of putting people in the right place at the right time, making sure the line moves smoothly, that the donations come in, that the leaks are fixed: mere mechanics, nothing more! Rusty looked squarely at me and made me realize this here is serious business, ultimately serious business.

When you are ordained, or confirmed, or baptized, indeed any time you receive sacramental grace—indeed, any time you receive communion at any altar—you are open to something that may feel like being let down. As you become stronger and draw closer to God, you become more of a target for whatever is evil in the world. It is not only in a context of avowed enemies of Christ that we might experience that attack. It can happen right in the church.

What then shall we do? Obviously, we don't want to avoid receiving grace! It won't do to say: well, I might feel let down or attacked, so I won't get baptized (or receive communion, or be confirmed). It has helped me, these past twenty-five years since I entered seminary, to remember Rusty's firm belief that we can be the object of spiritual attack. But he could say that only because he further believed the reality (which is stronger than any feeling) that God has already won the victory over every evil. After all, why do we call sacraments "grace"? Because they convey to us the victory of Jesus over death. Jesus is alive: it is the grace of the Holy Spirit to give us the living Jesus in the water of baptism, the bread and wine of the altar, and in the laying on of hands in confirmation. Whatever you may sense in the midst of a sacrament, it is the living Jesus who is coming to you with love and power.

The Xerox Machine[1]

T HE BIG MACHINE in our parish offices is the xerox that resides in the fifth floor hallway. This is the brawn of our office, the heavy-lifter, the multi-tasker, the competent aide we count on for just about everything. When I want a good or quick printout of a document, I send it there. When Douglas, the rector's secretary, wants a hundred copies of the nine o'clock leaflet (legal-sized paper, folded in half), he sends it there. The weekly prayer list, the rector's sermons for the narthex, education brochures (often an eight-page booklet, folded from two colored letter sheets printed on both sides, and stapled), music booklets for the choir (large eleven-by-seventeen-inch paper, double-sided print, folded), even the quarterly rector's chronicle (also eleven-by-seventeen, double-sided, folded, of which we used to print

---

1   Please note that I use "xerox" as a lower-case, common noun. This is how language works naturally: someone invents a new thing, and being the first or the most prominent early developer, the name becomes the name for the group. I blow my nose on kleenex, my pants have a zipper, and I sometimes take an aspirin. Indeed, where I grew up, the word "coke" itself was generic for a soft drink, leading to such absolutely delightful questions as "What kind of coke do you want? We've got Coke, Dr. Pepper, 7-Up…" I would think that, if they had any brains, Coca-Cola International Corporation Limited and Amalgamated would be pleased that their word, and thus their product, was the template standard for all.

three thousand copies): our faithful machine produces them all. This book itself, some two hundred pages in manuscript, was printed there before I sent it to the editor.

We demand many complicated tasks of the xerox, but for all its brawn it of course has no brain. It is, although we tend to forget it, only a machine. But to complicate things, it doesn't always work. Indeed, this machine seems to delight in not working.

So you're walking through the hallway, going perhaps from Ann's office to Douglas's, and there is Kevin peering into the innards of the thing. He's got doors open, some internal part in his hand, another part is sticking out. "Jammed again?" you say; and he, "Seems to be, but I can't find stuck paper anywhere." Or it might be after five, and there's Judith, a stack of neatly folded copies to one side of her, but the machine is still, and she is kneeling before it. "Genuflecting again?" you say. It is not impossible to imagine Judith or even Angel worshiping the xerox; when they kneel in front of it, they are often quiet, as if lost in meditation. Not so Douglas: when he is near the machine, there's a constant growl of dissatisfaction and distrust, occasionally erupting into a rapid volcanic flow of invective. They have heard him all the way down to the first floor. Honest.

I say the xerox has no brain, but when it isn't working one wonders if it doesn't have a will of its own. It seems to possess an innate perversity. Maybe it has a demon? Perhaps we need a rite of exorcism?

The ancient gods were like our modern machines: things in the world that could help us but which could also turn upon us, and which demanded sacrifices from us. Zeus, Baal, Mercury, Poseidon, they were nothing but co-inhabitants of the universe with us, capable of helping or harming us, bearing intentions benevolent or malevolent, demanding from us time or gold or blood. You worshiped them, or else. In our technological sophistication, we believe we have left such ancient and superstitious god-worship behind. And in fact, with regard to those ancient gods, we have. The blood of babies is no longer given up to Molech. But there is a dangerous place in the human heart that longs for the secret by which we can control the world, at any cost. The old gods are dead, yet we have many new ones in their place. The gross national product. The cure of all disease. The conquest of death. Power over the wind, the stars, and the atom. Power to shape the future of the human race.

The word that encompasses many of our modern gods is "technology." This is not to say that technology is bad; no vast and multi-faceted cultural phenomenon like technology is simply either good or bad. What's there is a tendency, an element of our technological experience, something ancient that has never gone away but appears ever in new forms. It is the desire to have gods to worship, in order that we may control our existence. This is idolatry: and it is just as much a reality in twenty-first century New York as it was in seventh-century BC Palestine.

I've genuflected before the xerox, as we all have, and it is only a joke to call that posture "genuflection." But like all jokes, it points to something that's real.

The Lost Image

THE BLIND ARGENTINIAN POET and critic Jorge Luis Borges wrote a short "parable" about the lost face of God ("Paradiso, XXXI, 108," in his book *Labyrinths*). We all sense, he says, that something infinite in the world has been lost. And when we hear stories of people who have had a vision of God, a longing is stirred from somewhere deep inside us. Who does not long to see the face of God? Borges suggests that it's because we don't know God's face that we live with doubt; if we could but see God, then all our doubts would disappear.

And yet the truth is stranger. In a narrative twist that is characteristic of Borges's genius, he considers there may be a reason that we have lost God's face. Perhaps his image has been destroyed so that at any moment we can wonder if we might be seeing it. For instance: "A Jew's profile in the subway is perhaps that of Christ; the hands giving us our change at a ticket window perhaps repeat those that one day were nailed to the cross by some soldiers." Indeed, it might be that we are always seeing something of God. "Perhaps some feature of that crucified countenance lurks in every mirror; perhaps the face died, was obliterated, so that God could be all of us."

In a city of eight million, there must be thousands of people who are the same height as Christ, and thousands whose hair color is the same as his. The shape of his eyebrow, the line of his nose, the thickness of his lips: such features are shared among us already; why would we not be seeing his? Think of the thousands of small individual details of your body: your fingernails, the shape of a toe, the line of your neck, your hairline. Might not one of those tiny features be the same as his? And even if that is not the case, think of the thousands of people you might see on any day on sidewalk or bus or subway or elevator. Does it not seem likely that at least one of them would have one of his features, however small it might be?

As Christians we are committed to believing that every person is in some way identified with Christ. This belief follows from the doctrine of the Incarnation, that the Word of God took on human flesh and became fully human, in order to share our condition and redeem us from sin which destroys our humanity. As an oft-quoted sentence from the Vatican II document on the church in the modern world puts it: "by virtue of his Incarnation, the Son of God has united himself in some fashion with every human being." According to Christian conviction, every human being is in some way united to Jesus.

What Borges's parable puts before us is the imaginative possibility that our union with Christ might have as its witness physical signs. Although I do not think it is a fully adequate image of the Ascension to think of Christ as thereby "marinating" himself into the world—I think it is necessary for us to say that Christ has taken his human body into the Godhead itself—nonetheless Borges's is a very suggestive thought, that since the tomb was empty, since indeed the body of Christ is no longer anywhere on earth, we might be seeing his body at any moment in our lives. When you look in the mirror, when you notice the hand holding the door, when you glimpse a pair of eyes darting past you, when you see hair sticking out from under a cap: at any moment you may be seeing something of what Christ looked like.

Our human dignity, of course, is not in our looks. But if in every human being there might be something that looks of Christ, that is a sign of the truth that in every human being there resides the dignity that was restored when he came down from heaven to be one of us.

Sprinkled Faith

T HERE IS A PLACE IN HEBREWS (12:18ff.) where the writer gives
us a masterly piece of the rhetoric of contrast. We are told that
you have not come to this and this and this, but rather you have come
to these other things. In the first part of the contrast are images of
fear and dread: *a blazing fire, darkness, gloom, a tempest, a trumpet
blast*; and then he gets specific: *a voice whose words made the hearers
entreat that no further messages be spoken to them.* I think we can intuit
what the writer means; there is a kind of holiness that is frightening,
off-putting, fear-inducing; you have not come, he says, to hear a voice
so bone-chillingly terrible you would plead never to hear it again. On
the other side are images of heaven and fellowship and God. You have
come, he says, among other things, to *the heavenly Jerusalem, angels,
the assembly of those who are enrolled in heaven, to* the God of the universe, and *to Jesus.* And in parallel to the mention of Jesus the writer
puts: *the sprinkled blood that speaks more graciously than the blood of
Abel.* Hang on to that last line. Rather than coming to a god who is
awe-ful, you have come to the God who is grace-ful; not to a god who
would demand the still-pulsing heart of a virgin sacrifice, but the God
whose own heart has bled so that the cycle of blood-feud may cease for
ever. It is not the blood of Abel that we come to, crying out for revenge,

but the blood of Jesus, pleading for forgiveness, for peace. Truly, *his sprinkled blood speaks graciously.*

Yet I'd bet large sums of money that very few (if any) people, when they come into a church, are thinking about sprinkled blood. What are the reasons that people come to Saint Thomas? Lots come for special musical programs, a procession, a conference, a liturgical festival. Some others come because their sons are singing, and still others because friends are singing. Some are regulars who know the Anglican tradition of choral music and wish to experience it yet again. But we are on Fifth Avenue, where thousands of people walk by every hour, and for some of them it's just something about the door or the sign or the façade that draws them in, and they soak up the wonderful coolness and quiet and beauty. However they come and whoever they are, once they are in the church the reason they came doesn't matter. As Eliot would teach us (and as Hebrews suggests), our reasons for coming are not the reason we came, and what one thought one came for is not what one will find.

It was in the springtime some thirty-plus years ago, as I returned to my dorm after dinner, the sun still atop the Rocky Mountains to the west behind me, that I was aware that God had snuck up on me. I had been studying various things and talking a lot to many friends, as one does in college, but now there was a reality to all those things about God that I had mouthed for so many years. I had not not expected God to show up, and yet there he was. He had snuck up on me, and it was...okay.

So I think does faith come upon many people, like a cat from behind that starts to rub your leg; it is a pull on the cuff of your sleeve, a slight quickening of the heartbeat, the bead of water that forms in the corner of your eye. Something that's not exactly in the music but right beside it, something faintly smelled, something tugging, O so gently tugging. Such faith as may be finding you is not your accomplishment. Faith is not something we have managed to pull off. Nor is it a bold declaration of impersonal doctrine. Faith is a personal orientation to the truth, an alignment of the senses, a finding of our place in an assembly we had not expected. Perhaps it was music or a planned event or a friend or one knows not what that brings one to a site like Saint Thomas, but what we are all really looking for is a place in the great assembly praising God. God does not demand faith of us, unmusically. There is nothing harsh about faith. It comes upon us from the God who lived a human life so that we could learn celestial harmony.

He gently invites us. I often say that from the Cross God's love is poured out over the whole world. But perhaps the image of pouring is too heavy, or even smothering. Let us take the word from Hebrews: it is *sprinkled*, faith is. Faith is like dew on the altar, a gift gently dropped upon us with the sprinkled blood of Christ.

Ashes

WE HAVE THREE LITURGIES on Ash Wednesday. That's not surprising: we're on Fifth Avenue, we're a big church, we ought to have three liturgies. Two of them are sung by the full choir of men and boys. That, too, is not surprising: we should put out our best effort to launch the season of Lent. But I was warned. "People will be coming in all day long. For ashes. You've never seen anything like it."

Indeed I hadn't. Each of us clergy is assigned a couple of hours during the day in which we are to sit in a chair at the front of the nave, just below the chancel steps. Beside us is a small table with a bowl of ashes, and an old worn out chalice purificator to wipe our thumb— not clean; it will take a couple of weeks before all the black ash comes out of the ridges of the thumbprint. We wear a cassock, surplice, and purple stole; the surplice too will need washing by the end of this.

And the people come, about a hundred or a hundred fifty an hour; not a steady flood, but a continuous ebb and flow. I recognize only a few of them. Most of our congregation will want to come to one of the services, where they can receive ashes *and* the Eucharist, and hear the choir. These folk want the ashes.

They enter from Fifth Avenue through our narthex. Some go immediately to a pew and kneel. Others walk slowly up the center aisle, then turn into a pew. The church is silent and awesome, the only sounds those of feet on stone and kneeling cushions sliding and the squeak of wood.

And, when someone comes to me, my voice. When they get close I stand, mark the cross on their forehead with ash, and say, "Remember, O man, that dust thou art, and unto dust shalt thou return."

But just to say those words and nothing else seems both to them and me unbearably impersonal. And so many of them, before I say anything, greet me with a "Hello, Father." And after the words of imposition, they'll make a sign of the cross and I'll say "Peace" or "Peace be with you," and they often say "Peace." We do not hug or shake hands, however.

I think the oddest response to the words of imposition—which are, after all, a reminder of our mortality—is one that is surprisingly often given: "Thank you, Father." I've just told someone that he is going to die, and he thanks me! You wouldn't say that to your doctor, would you? Yet they come, single people, pairs, families, groups from work, blue collar, executive, artsy—throughout the day they come, without ceasing, to receive this dirty mark on the head, the sign that says to the world not the forbidden boasting "I am fasting; I am a good person" (cf. Matt. 6:16) but rather, "I am a Christian; I acknowledge I am going to die." Sometimes the ash falls from my thumb onto their nose or cheek or their dress or shirt. That too is a sign: mortality is not neat, not to be controlled. To a hundred or two hundred people I say, *remember, you are going to die.*

Some of my friends think it superstition; the trend amongst churches, indeed, is not to offer ashes except during the liturgies of the day. It even may be that most of the people who "get ashed" at Saint Thomas do not understand the meaning of "dust thou art." But

I wouldn't stop doing it. Brian Davies, the Dominican scholar, once told of distributing ashes beside an old tottering priest who couldn't remember the words. That priest was going from forehead to forehead saying, "This won't hurt, and it might do some good."

Max

THE REPORTS ARE THAT he had been his usual jocular self at that Wednesday's staff meeting. He had a lunch engagement with two others—it was to be their annual celebration of their sobriety—and so he went for his daily gym workout a bit early. He was found collapsed in the weight room, and pronounced dead on arrival at the hospital.

The shock to the parish was seismic. Our verger, Max, was forty-six—we kept saying, *only* forty-six. He was a picture of health, of energy. He solved problems more than he caused them. He had a delightful, multi-faceted personality. He was so very much a part of the life of our parish, particularly for the staff. And suddenly...

"Victor, I'm sorry to bother you on your vacation..." The voice was Jonathan's. He stammered a bit about the staff meeting, the gym, the hospital; then he said it plain. "Max is dead." What? "Victor, Max is dead." You could feel the shock, the love, the pain in the voice. The next morning I rang the church to leave a message for Douglas. Claudette answered—Claudette, whose voice always has an upbeat pitch, was flat. Did she say, "Good morning, Saint Thomas"? Or was it just, "Saint Thomas"? I don't remember. I spoke to Charles a bit later. "I just can't believe it." We shared a few memories.

Saturday, back in New York, the soup kitchen volunteers were preparing to go out on their delivery routes, and Betty offered an extra prayer for Max. There was much soberness in greeting each other that day, the need to be together. I stopped in the sacristy and there was the rector, vested for the mass. Before any words were said, we hugged.

The really awful thing about death is that we can no longer touch. And that's why, when someone dies, it is our good instinct to gather around each other. Eddie, Francena, James, Jesse, Stella, Frank, Rose, Warren: how good it is to see them! How good to be able to touch their arm, to see their eyes, to hear their voice! But Max, where is Max? Why isn't he here?

He wasn't there, we learned later, because of an aortic aneurysm, undetected, unknown, a fatal weakness hidden within his flesh. But this "answer" only raised more questions. Why did he have that? Where did that aneurysm come from? Could it have been fixed? Could it have been avoided? And down we went, down the path of dangerous questions.

The most dangerous of which is: what about me? It is the unavoidable ego question. Not: what will Max's death mean to me as a member of Saint Thomas's staff? That question can be answered by the good self-discipline that Max would have modeled for us: we will each work harder and pull together and do the best we can. No, the dangerous ego question is different. It is this: what is the fatal flaw in my body? What is it that I'm carrying around, and I don't know about it, and it will be the cause of my death?

It's a dangerous question, because to ponder it correctly means death to our own ego. There is something in me which will finally give out, and I will then die—barring, of course, an accident coming upon me sooner. Every one of us is mortal. The plaque with our name on it will have two dates. Sometimes the difference between those dates is very small. Other times, it can be more than a hundred years. Sometimes you are blessed, as the psalmist says, to see your children's children. Other times, it is a father who buries his child.

Charles had said, "I just can't believe it." None of us could. And none of us knew what we would do without Max. Yet, actually, we did know what we would do. We would have a funeral. Prayers would be said, hymns sung, and the body of Max commended to his maker. This is a great gift of the church, that we don't have to invent things to do when we die. The church has been here before.

Because, of course, someone else has been here before. And he lived even fewer years than Max's forty-six. He died, but in such a way that, in a strange image, he swallowed up death. "Death has been swallowed up," we say.

The night before the funeral, I had the 5:30 mass. During the prayers I became aware of someone standing in the aisle to the side of the altar. It turned out to be Joshua, one of the choir boys, who had left the choir supper early to come for communion. "The Body of Christ," I was shortly saying to him, as I placed the host in his small hands. Afterwards, with damp eyes, he was stammering apologies for being late. *"How are you, Joshua?"* I said.

"Fine," he answered, with a question-mark in his voice.

"It's really sad," I said, and he nodded. With his own eyes now damp, the priest embraced the boy, touched deeper than words over the love that had drawn him there, to kneel, to swallow—what is it? What is it we call it, so very paradoxically, this manna for mortals? Is it not, "the Bread of Life"?

Palm Mercy

I N MATTHEW CHAPTER 21, we see Jesus angry, with vigor driving out the sellers and the buyers within the temple and throwing over the money-changers' tables. His intention is to make the temple what the prophesies of old had called it: a house of prayer. He will reclaim the temple from thieves and thievery and purify it for God's purposes.

All the Gospels know Jesus did this angry and righteous and quite frighteningly holy act, even if they can't agree on the time of its happening. John puts it almost at the beginning of Jesus' ministry, whereas Mark puts it on the day after Jesus' triumphant entry into Jerusalem. If we used anachronistic shorthand and said that Jesus entered Jerusalem triumphantly on "Palm Sunday," then Mark says he cleansed the temple on "Holy Monday," and John says he did it a couple of years ago.

Matthew, however, says he did it on what we call Palm Sunday, on the same day that he was greeted with palms and hosannas by the crowds. For Matthew, the cleansing of the temple is the climax of Palm Sunday. And why is that? Here is the moment I'd like you to remember. Immediately after Jesus drove the buyers and sellers out, Matthew says, *the blind and the lame came to him in the temple, and he healed them.* And that's not all. *The children [were] crying out in the temple,*

"Hosanna to the Son of David!" Right in the middle of the story of Jesus cleansing the temple, on the same day that the crowds acclaimed him on the road, the blind and the lame and children came to him in the temple.

The blind and the lame and the little, overlooked people are the folks who came to Jesus throughout his ministry. He healed them and he welcomed them. Let us remember that Matthew's is the gospel of mercy. Matthew, as a despised tax collector, knew personally what it means to be shunned and hated, and he knew from Jesus what it means to receive mercy. So Matthew teaches us all those great stories of mercy, from Joseph at the beginning having mercy on Mary before he understands the meaning and the origin of her pregnancy, to many parables of rich people and powerful people who showed mercy (or who didn't), to the great parable of the final judgment, when people who have fed the hungry and visited the sick and done other acts of mercy are told, to their surprise, that every kind act ever done is an act done to Jesus.

Now here it is, right in the temple itself: mercy, in the persons of the blind and the lame, being healed by Jesus, and the young people, having been welcomed to Jesus, singing his praise. Mercy has set up shop in the heart of the temple. Which is of course where mercy belongs.

All this is for us a (sort of) picture of Jesus himself. *Destroy this temple*, Jesus said, *and in three days I will raise it up*. And he was destroyed, killed in a most brutal way, but then raised to new life on the third day. That Jesus whom we see on the cross, who was buried in the tomb, who slept in death and who rose to new life, he *is* the temple: in his heart he carries the blind and the lame, and all the little people, and everyone who joins the crowd saying hosanna. And all the people who have ever longed for mercy, he has a place cleared for them in his heart, *a place for you and for me*, a place of mercy and healing and joy and song. I suppose that the question for us every year as we embark upon Holy Week is this. Will we come to that cleansed-out place in the heart of the temple? Will we draw closer to the place Jesus has prepared for us?

Washing Feet

IT SURPRISED ME, the first time I was on the receiving end of the ceremonial foot washing, how pleasant and cool it felt. Our feet endure a lot down there, as Garrison Keillor's ditty puts it, "from your ankles to your toes, at the bottom of your clothes." Feet carry our weight through the day, squeezed into shoes much of the time, sweating, ignored. They benefit us continually, yet we tend to take them for granted. So although it was slightly embarrassing (I don't normally take off my shoes in church), I found the foot washing to be relaxing, and tender, and just plain good.

When Jesus refreshes his disciples' feet, the scene is intimate. It is also unusual: feet were washed not in the midst of a meal, but upon arrival in a home. And they were washed by their owner: a thoughtful host would present you with water to wash your own feet. No one would be expected to wash another's feet; even slaves, or at least Hebrew slaves, could not be commanded to do as much. (For details, see Raymond Brown's commentary on the Gospel of John.) But here is Jesus himself performing the act, humble service, humiliating service, unexpectedly.

It is, he tells them afterwards, an example for all his followers to follow, that we should serve one another with humility, loving one another as he has loved us. Disciples of Jesus should treat each other with the same tender care that Jesus gave to the apostles' feet. Your neighbor may be something like the "feet" that support a heavy burden, some burden she has to carry; others may take her for granted. She may find herself, as it were, squeezed into a situation that's tight and difficult much of the day. Don't ignore her, and don't be rough on her. Find the cool water that will refresh her, Jesus says; love her as I have loved you.

Yet the love of Christians for one another is not the end of the meaning of the foot washing, nor is it even the most important thing to say. And the reason is that Jesus is never merely an example for us. Christianity is not first about what we do or should do, but about what God does. Jesus washing the disciples' feet is a prophetic action.

The prophetic action begins when he takes off his outer garments. The scripture uses the verb *lays aside. He laid aside his garments*, John writes. And when Jesus is done, he takes them up again: *When he had washed their feet, [he took] his garments*. Please think with me here of how Jesus speaks about his death. It is the same verb: *I lay down my life*. And after he has died: *I take it up again* (John 10:17 etc.). Jesus removing his garments in order to wash their feet in the middle of the meal is a prophecy in deeds, not in words, that points to his death very soon to come. And it is a sign also of the humiliating character of his death. The baseness of washing feet prefigures the humiliation of exposure on the cross.

In other gospels, when Jesus utters prophetic words and tells his disciples that he will die, Peter brusquely refuses to accept it. *God forbid it, Lord*, he says. Similarly here in John, Peter refuses to accept the prophetic action of Jesus washing his feet. *You shall never wash my feet*, Peter says, which means, being interpreted, *you shall not die, you shall not be so humiliated.* To which Jesus answers: *If I do not [do this], you have no part in me.* The humiliation of Jesus even unto death is necessary if he is to be our savior, if we are to have any "part" in him. This night, in the intimacy of the upper room, it is a pageant of symbol and mystery. The next day on the cross it is brutally real.

He lays aside his life for us, and he will take it up again. But it is no light thing for Jesus to lay aside his garments. It puts him down there, down below us, down at our feet, doing something that is so degrading it makes him almost subhuman. But then he puts on his garments, and he is lifted up, and we have a part in him.

On Good Friday we confront the pain, nails pounded into nerves, asphyxiation, abandonment, the cruciform reduction of a human being to just so much flesh. And it is important to face that, to see how far he was willing to go. But let us remember—will you remember with me?—that painful as it is for him, at the same time that our hearts break for him, we simultaneously feel the unexpected coolness and gentleness, like water on the feet, the touch that washes away our tiredness and despair, and gives us hope for life. He is dying, and we are being tenderly held. *Having loved his own who were in the world, he loved them*—he loved us—*to the end.*

Betrayal

ONE OF YOU WILL BETRAY ME. So spoke Jesus to his twelve closest friends. It is just after supper, what will turn out to have been the last meal of his life. During that supper he had washed their feet—twelve men, twenty-four feet, washed them all, showing them that he was not only their teacher, but their servant. Yet this servant, this Jesus, he knows everything. There have been signs all along showing that Jesus knows what is in the human heart. *One of you will betray me*, he says; and he knows who it is.

But the friends of Jesus, they do not know who it is. Might it be that one? Or that one? They start looking at one another in a new way. Which of them might it be? *The disciples looked at one another, uncertain.* Each of them may have wondered, not only which of these others might do it, but, Am I the one? Might Jesus be speaking about me? Am I going to betray him?

Jesus knows, but they don't. It is important for us to realize that the "Judas possibility" exists inside every human heart. Suppose circumstances change; for the sake of money—or (even more seductively) for the sake of a good cause, if you became persuaded that your erstwhile friend had gone seriously astray and had turned his back on his great chance—might you not betray him? Can you be certain you wouldn't?

The disciples looked at one another, uncertain. But Jesus, who knows the human heart, knows that most of them will not betray him, although they might; he knows the one who will—who, indeed, has already set the machinery of the state in motion. To him he hands a dipped morsel. That one goes out. It is night.

Immediately Jesus says a peculiar thing. His betrayer has gone out to do his work quickly, and Jesus declares, *Now is the Son of man glorified.* This is his hour, the point of his life, his lifting-up, his self-offering, his love poured out over the world like a river of life, gently flowing, springing from the cross and moving inexorably to every patch of earth, so that there are no feet anywhere in the world that will not feel the cool cleansing of that water. Because Jesus is betrayed, Jesus is glorified.

All the feet of the world that are touched by the life-water that flows from the cross, they receive that water only because Jesus was glorified. And Jesus was glorified only because he was betrayed. It is key to this story that every disciple was uncertain who would turn Jesus in. It is equally key for each of us to comprehend that we also might have betrayed him. For if betrayal is impossible, so is salvation.

You have perhaps been betrayed, at one time or another, by someone you had counted as your friend. I say "perhaps," because although I hope it hasn't happened to you, it seems to happen to most people. Humans are the creatures who love, and who betray. And what do we get when we are betrayed?

Might it be that we find Jesus?

On Good Friday

A T THE END OF THE DAY what we have is a corpse. His muscles no longer move; his brain cells issue no commands; there is not the slightest movement in his chest; the blood no longer circulates; his flesh is cold as stone, and there it is, lying in chill darkness, closed over and put away.

At the end of the day we begin to realize that we will never again hear his voice. He will not tell us another of his stories. We won't walk alongside him on the road; we won't find him across from us at table. And we know that we are only just beginning to feel the enormity of our loss.

At the end of the day we have terrible memories. There is guilt. He had so much to tell us, and we were asleep. He had shared his soul with us, but when it got dangerous, we ran away. And there is nightmare: the brutality of what was done to him! The shame of his nakedness; the whip, the thorns in his scalp; the sneers. Nails through nerves; dehydration; suffocation. These images in our memory of torture and abandonment: how will we ever get over them?

At least the pain is over now. Yet it's *all* over, isn't it. All that's left of his voice, his vitality, his dream—all that's left, at the end of the day, is this corpse.

Yes and no.

As the stun of it settles in, the mind goes back and starts to tarry over some small bits of remembrance, things not noticed earlier, but now recalled, noticed particularly by our friend, the theologian John. Did you see how he was calm through it all? He knows he will be betrayed; calmly he states this truth at supper. He goes to the garden; there his betrayer comes with an arresting party. He addresses them with authority: *Whom do you seek?* And hearing the name, he replies without a twitch: *I AM,* and it is not he but those who would seize him who fall to the ground. Pilate, in the middle of his interrogation, has him scourged; when he comes back, in that ghastly beaten shape with thorns and purple upon him, still he is master of himself. *Where are you from?* Pilate asks, adding *Do you not know that I have power to release you?* His voice remains sure: *You would have no power over me unless it had been given you from above.*

The recollection of his calmness starts to wax in our minds. Then it occurs to thought that he remained strong to the end. He carried his own cross—even scourged and beaten as he was. And with that strength of body there was strength of character. He knew what was happening right to the end. In fact, even though he was the victim, he seemed somehow to be in charge of the situation. As if, even though they were killing him, he was choosing to allow himself to die. Did he not end it all by saying, *It is finished?*

He was calm and strong to the end, and although many of us ran away, not all of us did. He had said to Pilate, *Every one who is of the truth hears my voice.* Even there, nailed and hanging in the torture of drawn-out capital punishment, he was taking care of his mother and his friends. He made a new family, right there, right at the foot of the cross: *Woman, behold, your son!* And to the disciple: *Behold, your mother!* We had thought of his dying as isolation and abandonment, but now it seems quite the contrary: as he was dying, he created new community.

His self-possession to the end, his strength, his loving provision for his friends: all this shows us that Good Friday is the effectuation of kingship. When they nailed him to the cross, they put him upon his throne. There he did what from the beginning he had been prepared to do: he became the ruler of the universe. Lifted on high, he became king, drawing to himself all who hear his voice.

At the end of the day, yes, we have a corpse. But not only a corpse. On this day a kingdom has been brought into being. Which is to say, we have a good Friday.

Avery

ONE OF THE "READERS" of my dissertation was Avery Dulles, a Jesuit priest, the theologian author of a shelfful of books, and at that time a distinguished professor at Fordham University. I first met him when, as a new doctoral student, I wrote a paper on the ecclesiology of the full-communion agreement between the Lutheran and Episcopal churches. He wasn't my professor, but I knew he was an expert in ecumenism; he had, in addition, a reputation of being generously available to graduate students. So I made bold to ask, and he was glad to read my paper; a few days later he met with me to discuss it. Sister Anne-Marie, his longtime assistant, brought me coffee; I nearly disappeared into a deep comfortable chair; and he sat, in his utilitarian desk chair, surrounded by books, sipping water.

In January I signed up for his course on Newman's fundamental theology. There were four of us in that graduate seminar. He made us each responsible for thirty minutes of class time every week, presenting summaries and response papers to various works of Newman's. It was demanding: although we enjoyed the class, we worked harder for him than for any other professor.

I recall the first meeting of that seminar. Father Dulles had slipped on the ice at the university over the holidays and had broken his arm. He appeared without a tie, in a sports jacket, and told us that he was in a quandary. Should he, as a Jesuit, sue the university, or as a member of the university, should he sue the Jesuits? He gave a light chuckle. Later that term it happened that our class fell on April 1. Father Dulles began by wishing us a happy feast. "Feast?" I thought. It was still Lent, and it certainly wasn't the feast of the Annunciation. He grinned and said, "Feast of fools!"

It was on April 1, 2008, more than a decade later, that the now-Cardinal Dulles was scheduled to give his final address as the McGinley professor of religion and society at Fordham. The auditorium was full of students and priests, faculty and townspeople, when the backstage curtain behind the podium and desk parted slightly and Cardinal Dulles was rolled in. Now in a wheelchair, erect with strong jaw under tight skin, he looked from side to side, taking us in. Not a word had yet been spoken, and yet we were all on our feet, giving him our applause.

We were told that he was not able to speak. During the reception, we were informed, he would be glad to greet us, but we were not to ask him for a blessing or to try to kiss his cardinal's ring; his right side was not under his control. Still he had written his lecture, which was delivered by the president emeritus, Father O'Hare. It was an account of his life, his twenty-year tenure at Fordham, his theological convictions, his understanding of how a theologian should "think with" the church. It was also deeply moving, particularly at the end.

Through Father O'Hare's occasionally quaking voice, Avery Dulles told us that he had contracted polio when he was in military service in 1945. For most of his life its effects were not bothersome, but now at the end he no longer was able to speak or move his side. I thought back to the last few times I had seen him, and remembered a limp that he had had over the last decade. But his descent into muteness had come about in less than two years. I looked down at the stage: the brilliant elderly Cardinal-theologian-priest, sitting in wheelchair at desk, listening to the voice of the past university president reading his words. Now he was saying that he had no regrets. He reminded us of the last years of Pope John Paul II, who had said it was necessary that the pope should suffer. Cardinal Dulles said he now identified himself with the many people who were mute or invalid in the world and particularly in the gospel stories. There was not, in his speech, the slightest hint of anger or frustration or even sadness. This is what it means to be human. And I thought: this is what it means to be a great student of the ways of God.

Perhaps the church will name him among the saints in the years to come. But his wit, as I write this, is still with him. After Father O'Hare finished reading the lecture, after the applause died down, Cardinal Dulles asked for a notepad. He wrote, and the audience became quite silent. Father O'Hare picked up the pad, and laughed. "What he has written isn't true," O'Hare said into the microphone; "he writes: 'Thanks for improving the lecture.'" We all laughed as the cardinal looked at us, his eyes twinkling.

Avery Cardinal Dulles died peacefully on December 12, 2008, at the age of ninety.

Good-bye for Now

WHEN THE RECTOR AND I went to Saint Patrick's Cathedral for the funeral of Avery Dulles, we wanted to sit to the side and towards the back, in case we had to leave before the ceremony was over. But it was not to be. The rector, you see, is a well-known person. So when we asked an usher for a program, she said, "You're Father Mead," which he couldn't deny, and she said, "Come with me," and she took us up the left side aisle to the very front of the nave. We parked our coats and slid into the pew. A few minutes later the family was being brought into church, along with the casket; they came down towards us from the ambulatory that goes around the sanctuary, and as the procession passed in front of us, the cathedral's rector turned to my rector and said: "I have a seat for you." A few minutes later he had moved us to the opposite side, still at the very front, but now directly before the magnificent pulpit. This was the seating reserved for ecumenical clergy.

When the hour had come for the service to begin, there was a vast procession of Catholic clergy: deacons, priests, bishops, archbishops, and cardinals. One of them looked very ill. In fact, I had heard he was in bed with cancer, and so I was surprised to see him. He saw me and nodded in recognition. His name was Richard John Neuhaus, and this funeral of his friend was, as it turned out, the last public appearance he made before his own death not many weeks later.

During the funeral service, good hymns were sung; recognition of Avery's protestant past was given; the archbishop of New York delivered himself of a superb homily. Scripture and ceremony combined to convey the Christian hope amidst the sorrow of death. Much of it was moving to all who were present; from my seat at the front, however, I found most moving the things that happened at the end.

After communion, the burial mass concludes with a ceremony that occurs around the coffin, which throughout the service has been placed in the front of the center aisle. It is censed and sprinkled with holy water, and the pall is removed, revealing the polished wood with the crucifix on its top. When this had been done for Avery Dulles, after the archbishop said the final prayers, all the Catholic clergy processed out, down the long center aisle to the front Fifth Avenue doors; in doing so, all of them passed by Cardinal Dulles's casket. I started to notice that some of them were touching it as they passed. Not every priest or bishop did so; some just walked smartly on. But many did. It was as if they were saying, "This is my friend, my brother in Christ"; and although Avery could no longer be touched in the flesh—one could no longer squeeze his hand or touch his arm—he could be touched in this way one last time. A Jesuit priest from Fordham University made a small sign of the cross upon the casket as he passed by, and then crossed himself. Father Neuhaus touched the casket three times, as if he suspected he would soon be joining his friend on the farther shore.

When all the clergy had passed, the pall bearers took their places and lifted the casket up onto their shoulders. In this way they were able to carry it high, and without touching it with their hands. It was almost mystical, watching the casket slowly move west down the cathedral aisle, moving above the heads of all the people, seemingly moving on its own, a simple wooden casket. Spontaneously the people throughout the packed cathedral erupted in applause. Long, hearty, sustained applause, as the wooden box with the earthly remains of a prince of the church moved slowly, slowly towards the afternoon winter light of the open doors, moved as if in a pageant of symbols towards the Light that had made him and called him and redeemed him, and was now taking him home to rest.

Material Continuity

IT SEEMS TO ME THAT the older I get, the more a materialist I become. Here's a childhood memory. We're in Oklahoma, driving a couple hours back home from the funeral of one of my great aunts. And I'm saying to my parents, I don't see why people are sad at funerals. Aunt Velma has left her body behind and gone to be with Jesus. Shouldn't we be happy about that?

I suppose my picture of heaven at that time would have been one of clouds, wings, and harps. When we die, we become angels, or like angels; we escape from the world and rise to heaven to live with all the other good people who have died, and with God.

When I went to college I discovered that Christians did not believe what I thought they did. Rather, they (we) believe in the resurrection of the body. It was Socrates who peacefully drank the hemlock, telling his friends not to weep because his soul was being released from its prison. By contrast, Jesus wept at Lazarus's death. And when Jesus himself rose from death, he did so *bodily*—at least according to traditional Christianity. He ate fish. He told Thomas to touch his wounds.

But those resurrection stories, should we take them literally? At that time I would have said that I took them...seriously, but would have emphasized the wide range of the accounts of Jesus' resurrected body. For instance, besides his being able to eat and be touched, he was also able to appear in a room without coming through the door. That doesn't seem to be a physical or material body, I said. I would emphasize that to be human is to have a body; and thus, to have eternal life with God means to be a human with a new body that doesn't die or wear out, having eternal life with God. I had abandoned the notion that we escape from bodiliness. But surely our bodies change when we die. What would be the connection of our new body with the old? I didn't think there needed to be any connection.

Then one evening just a few years ago I was having dinner with Brian and he said I had it wrong. He said that Aquinas, at least, insists on "material continuity." That is, the resurrection body must be continuous, on the level of matter, with the earlier body. The rank materialism of the thought dumbfounded me. How can the body that is raised be connected—materially connected—with the body that died?

Of course, it came to me, *that's why Jesus' tomb was empty*: the resurrected Christ is the Christ that Peter and the Magdalene and the others had known. His body had changed, but it was precisely *his body* that had changed; he didn't throw away the old one (and leave it in the dump of the grave).

But why is it important that Jesus' tomb be empty? Why must we have material continuity?

Around this time, as I recall, the papers reported the uncovering of an elaborate hoax in the art world: a painting long attributed to a master turned out to have been a fake. From time to time one learns of paintings that were forgeries or hoaxes. The deception might be exposed by, for instance, carbon-14 dating that shows the canvas not to be from the period of the master, or chemical analysis of the paint that reveals it to be a sort of paint unknown in the master's time, or some other forensic evidence. But consider: suppose you have a Rembrandt. (I know, suppose you have a billion dollars. Well, why not? We're just *supposing*.) Now suppose you decide to make a copy of your Rembrandt that could never be detected as a copy. I would guess that within the next few decades it will become technologically possible to reproduce a Rembrandt in such a way that it is flat impossible to identify it as a copy rather than an original. It is only a matter of overcoming certain technical problems—and what our society does well is figuring out how to overcome technical problems. So now imagine that the deed is done. You have before you two indistinguishable Rembrandts: your original and your copy. There is absolutely no difference between them, save the fact that one was original and the other the copy. How do you tell the real thing from the fake? There is only one way. You have to tell the history: the real painting is the one Rembrandt executed, and it went from owner to owner until it came to you. The copy has no such history.

The difference, in other words, between the real painting and the fake is that the real painting has *material continuity*. It is material continuity that gives it its identity, its authenticity.

That's why we need our resurrection bodies to be *our* bodies: so that we can tell our personal story—our life story—as one story. Aunt Velma in heaven is the real Aunt Velma, and not a cloned substitute, thanks to the rank materialism of Christian faith.

Day of Our Lives

I T HAPPENS EVERY DAY. It is so common we almost never think about it. But look: the day begins. It is God's gift to us. We read in the Psalms: *This is the day which the Lord hath made*—this day, like every day. We rise from bed and give thanks to God—if we remember! And some days are great days, spectacular days. One Saturday after-noon you take a dear friend to Central Park. The daffodils are blooming everywhere. There are about a million people there—friendly, walking, amorous, athletic, speaking about forty different languages—it is so exciting. A woman pushes a stroller with a girl in it, and beside her a very short boy pushes a tiny stroller with Curious George in it. But then it comes to an end. The sun sets, and the day is over. And we give thanks—if we remember.

Our prayers encourage us to look at each day as our life in min-iature. Consider the beloved prayer for the evening, adapted from one by John Henry Newman: "O Lord, support us all the day long, until the shadows lengthen, and the evening comes, and the busy world is hushed, and the fever of life is over, and our work is done." It is a prayer of *trust in* God. The preposition is important. We aren't trusting *that* God will support us, nor merely trusting God to speak truly when he promises to support us. Rather, this is a prayer of commitment, of placement: at the end of the day we place our lives in God's hands, just as at the end of our days we will place our lives in his hands for ever. The prayer concludes: "Then in thy mercy, grant us a safe lodging, and a holy rest, and peace at the last."

"Think" and "thank" have a common root. To *think* of the day as God's creation is to *think through* the day to God as its maker and, thus, to *thank* God for the day. And as we cannot ask God to support us through the day without, at the end of the day, entrusting ourselves to him, so we cannot recollect the day as God's making without, also, thanking God when the gift comes to an end.

Each day is our life in miniature. The Curious George you saw on that gorgeous day in Central Park will, perhaps, make it through a few seasons. That very short boy who was pushing Curious George will grow tall, and perhaps some day you may find him pushing a larger stroller. He may later push a wheelchair. At length there will come the season when he no longer can take that walk. Then it will be over. And the question is, in what manner will he think of it all? Will he give thanks at the end?

Truly it is all ours—the earth, the flowers, the children, the excitement, the joy, the sun, the moon, and the stars. Not ours as King Nebuchadnezzar thought, who, standing on the roof of his Babylonian palace, said *Is not this great Babylon, which I have built by my mighty power...for the glory of my majesty?* (Dan. 4:30). It is not ours as our making or our glory, but ours as gift received. How can we not feel that gratefully? Yet evening will come, and they will all be taken away—the smells, the sights, the touch. Will we give thanks as they depart?

Every day God gives us everything. In the giving, God tries to bring us to himself. And at the end of the day, in the taking away, God tries to bring us to himself. Faith sees always gift—and praises the giver, who lives beyond the daffodils, the cries, the stars, beyond even the grave. For he is indeed the living God.

Chance Encounters

IT WAS EASTER MONDAY, a staff holiday at Saint Thomas, a day of blessed release after the "all-church, all-the-time" intensity of Holy Week. I thought I'd go to a museum, but choices are limited: almost every museum in New York closes on Monday. The exception is the Museum of Modern Art. (They are our neighbors on West 53rd Street. Strangers have sometimes asked me if I know where MOMA is. "Sure," I say with glinting eye, "it's right next to Saint Thomas Church.") So I was in MOMA, in casual civilian clothes, alone in a crowd and, I thought, anonymous. Just then a man touched my arm. "Good to see you, Father Austin. We loved the Easter service yesterday."

Memo to priests: You never know when you'll be seen. Don't count on anonymity.

I managed to go to my gym for more than a year without anyone knowing I was a priest. I even took a ballet class (good for humility). My teacher asked me once—it was maybe two years after I started—if I was a professor. "Used to be," I said; "I'm a priest." Cover blown. Then one evening a familiar bass voice said, "Hello, Father Austin." It was Steve, who sings in our choir. He not only has a great, deep voice, he also presses about four hundred pounds. I saw Steve at the gym off and on for a year, and never anyone else I knew, until a string of coincidences. First was a couple who introduced themselves to me as having recently come back to Saint Thomas; he had been in the youth group ten or twenty years ago. Then there was a man who had taken several of my Aquinas classes. And then, in one and the same evening, I saw both Angel, our facilities chief, and Fred, one of our organists.

People say New York is a city of small towns. Being a priest in New York is like being at the intersection point of many small towns simultaneously. Once I greeted a man at a midweek service; he was wearing a sweatshirt that said "Tulsa." "I'm from Oklahoma," I told him, "and my brother's wife grew up in Tulsa. 'America's most beautiful city,' they used to say." That was about all of our small talk, until Christmas Eve. I was shaking hands after the midnight mass when this middle-aged man and a younger man came to me. "I'm the guy with the Tulsa sweatshirt," he said, reminding me that we had met. Now he gave me his name, and he asked, as if he were checking, "Are you Father Austin?" It turns out that he had been married to a sister of my brother's wife. While they were married, back in my seminary days, my family had visited them in their New York apartment. I remember that they had a pet reptile that roamed their apartment freely, consuming cockroaches. (Seriously.) And this young adult beside him I had last seen as a toddler.

So what do we have here? The family circle, including in-laws and out-laws; Midtown Manhattan workers; the Christmas Eve crowds; the Oklahomans-in-exile. Family, work neighborhood, altar, and the home we came from, all intersect in unpredictable ways.

Another time I was walking up Broadway in the 70s or 80s and I passed an Italian man who used to come frequently to midday masses. It was surprising to see him in a different place, and I wasn't able to call up his name until he had passed by. The next winter, another encounter: I was at City Ballet, and at the end of the performance a man reached across a couple of people to touch my sleeve. He was there with his wife, both of them new to Saint Thomas, and they had just started attending the doctrine class. Then maybe two weeks later when I next went to the ballet, they had the seats immediately beside mine. What could be the odds of that?

Does God work through chance? I know many couples who met up again by sheer coincidence, but at a time in their life when it seemed it was fitting for them to do so, and they became good friends or even married. Chance encounters? Yes, from a human perspective. Yet if we believe that God is a living God, then we must hold that he has purposes, that there are things that God wants to get done. And if we are alert to it, if we live with a certain openness or attentiveness, then we may discover opportunities in the unexpected intersections of our lives, opportunities that God wants to give us.

I think God may be trying to teach me that I am more connected to other people than I like to think. Just days before writing this I was late for an appointment, rushing down a subway platform, when a man I had last seen in Hopewell Junction more than ten years ago, wearing a black suit but no tie, rose from the bench and stammered "Father Austin" and told me his name. Although I only knew him as a brief and casual attender of my old church in Dutchess County, I remembered him, and I thought, how strange that at this very moment we would both be on the platform, we who hadn't seen each other for a decade and had no reason to want to see each other. Just then the train pulled in and I had to squeeze on. I wonder if I'll see him again.

Cookbooks

S USAN LOVES TO READ, buy and collect cookbooks, even though, since her brain surgery, she hasn't been able to do much cooking. She likes to read them, just as she likes to read her beloved novels and mysteries and children's stories.

Apparently she is far from alone. A recent news article reported on the continued brisk sales of cookbooks, despite what the article claimed was their complete obsolescence. If you want to cook, say, risotto with sauteed shrimp, corn, and fresh basil, why, you open your computer and google it. Within seconds, the recipe is on your screen. Apart from classics like *The Joy of Cooking*, the article was telling me, cookbooks should be utterly passé.

In fact, as it went on to say, thanks to the economic downturn, people are more likely to cook a fancy meal for themselves than to go out to eat. The cost even of high-quality, unusual food for cooking is still less than the cost of going to a restaurant.

I suspect, however, that a lot of New Yorkers may be reading cookbooks but still going out to eat. They are different from normal people, New Yorkers are. Libby, while she was preparing the altar, once announced with disarming frankness: "I say, why eat at home when you can go out?" That's true New-Yorker-speak. A recent short essay by Joseph Epstein asked why there is such high quality of food in New York. Epstein says it comes from New Yorkers being so demanding about their food. Here's an example, more or less as he gave it: "I want a sardine sandwich on rye, lightly toasted, with a thin slice of onion—last time the onion was too thick—with a gentle rinse of lemon between the sardines and the onion. Pickle on the side." New Yorkers are demanding when it comes to food. We also approach an unfamiliar restaurant with open suspicion. Just last week I witnessed a New Yorker order a turkey club at Cassidy's. "Your turkey," she said, "it's fresh turkey, right?" Although the waitress said it was, my friend didn't look convinced. She ordered the club but reserved judgment.

What are we doing, then, when we read cookbooks, particularly if the computer has made them obsolete and also if, as determined New Yorkers, we're going to go out to eat anyway? One thing we might be doing, it seems to me, is theology.

I'm thinking in that way because for many years, decades really, there was a *New York Times* food critic who was an Episcopal priest who also wrote humorous books in theology. One that Susan and I have—in fact, for several years we had *two* copies, one in hardcover to keep and one in paperback to use—is called *The Supper of the Lamb*. It's a cookbook, but it has only a single recipe ("lamb for eight persons four times"). The author, Robert Farrar Capon, uses the book to reflect on food, love, the meaning of life, and everything. He tells us, for instance, that there was no reason for God to make the universe. God didn't have to be a creator, he would still have been God and been quite happy as such, thank you very much. Creation is completely gratuitous. The whole universe, Capon says, is like an orange peeling that's hanging on the chandelier in God's kitchen. He doesn't throw it away, he leaves it there, he lets it be, for no other reason than that he rather likes it.

One of the first things you have to do in *The Supper of the Lamb* is to cut an onion. Capon has you cut the onion in half, and then stop. Pause, he says, to notice a remarkable thing. If you take the two halves of a cut onion, they don't fit back together. Each half has swollen where you cut it, and sort of pushes itself out. (Go try it yourself, if you've never seen it.) Creation is full of surprises like that which we can rush through life and never notice: the onion half that wants to be, that pushes itself forward into the world. The universe is glad to exist.

Cookbooks, it seems to me, are natural places to look for theology; Robert Farrar Capon, theologian and food-writer, grabbed onto a deep connection of things. The kitchen, he would say, is midway between the slaughter-house and the altar. At the slaughter-house things are done that we don't often think about to turn animals into the meat that we take into our kitchens and prepare to eat. The kitchen, that is to say, is connected with the realities of our life as physical beings on earth; it is connected with the garden, the ranch, and the harvest of the sea. On the other side, the kitchen is half-way to the altar. On the altar the gifts of the earth are offered to God, who turns them into food for us, the real, sacramental food of Jesus who gives life to the world. The food of the altar unites us in spiritual communion with God and with each other. If we were beasts, we would eat raw, uncooked meat. If we were gods, we would commune with heavenly nectar only. But we are human, neither beast nor god, and that's why we have kitchens.

Water

THE ANCIENTS CONSIDERED IT, along with earth, air, and fire, to be one of the four constituent elements out of which everything was made. And although these days we know about way more than a hundred elements, and notwithstanding the discovery that every atom of every element can itself be broken into smaller and thus more elementary particles, water nonetheless remains essential to us humans. Our bodies, as we know, are mostly water, which suits us for living on this planet, which, exceptionally, has a surface that is mostly covered with water. By contrast, the universe at large is flat inhospitable to us, lacking for the most part even trace amounts of H_2O.

Cities can survive only when their water supply is assured, and that is a complex business. The small town where I grew up in Oklahoma had a water tower. It was fed by underground aquifers, the water being pumped into the huge towering tank, and then gravity delivering it to the people. A water tower is also a community center of sorts. It was good sport for high-school students at night to climb high and then paint on the side of it "Class of 78," say (not that I knew personally anyone who did such a thing). There were pipes to lay and maintain, and meters to run so that usage could be billed, and inspections to make sure the water remained pure, but it was not unimaginably complicated.

Even simpler is the system in place in East Fishkill, the town a bit upstate where I lived for many years. There each plot of land had its own well. Our parish had a well that supplied both the rectory and the church. It was very hard water, so we had to keep a water softener running, and that meant refilling a tank with fifty or eighty pounds of salt every few weeks. All of our neighbors had their own wells, and each of us, presumably, was drawing from the same underground source. As the town population was multiplying, there was concern that this system wouldn't last indefinitely. Still it was pretty clear how it worked, and apart from the occasional storm that knocked out power (not to mention the time our pump-head suffered a lightning strike) the costs were minimal.

Where then does New York City water come from, and how does it get to us? We are the beneficiaries of one of the greatest water-works projects in the world, laid out and constructed more than a century ago. Our water comes from beautiful reservoirs upstate, some of them in Westchester and Putnam counties, and more even further north in the Adirondacks. Our water is the snow in the New York mountains that melts and runs into streams and lakes in the spring. I've seen some of these lakes. There is an abandoned rail line that runs through Westchester up into Putnam, and you can walk or bike up this easy and level path. In northern Westchester county, the path goes across an old train bridge, suspended high above a glorious blue lake. You couldn't get there any other way, and the views are spectacular. You won't see lakeside houses or beaches, just trees right down to the water-line. *That's* the water we drink.

It is the best water in the world. That's not just my opinion; it's what John Granlund told me when he helped us move from seminary to Wappingers Falls, and he should know (he was a native and an IBM engineer). Okay, there might be good water where you live, and yes I might not have tasted it. But I know the water in Moscow (don't drink it), in London (okay), in Oklahoma (flat), in Dutchess County (hard, see above), and in Santa Paula, California (made me sick). When you're in a restaurant here in New York and the waiter asks you if you'd like bottled or tap water, you should speak boldly. "I'd like New York City tap water." Then look him in the eye and say, "It's the best water in the world."

I'm tempted to say: If you're thirsty, come to New York. We have an immensely complicated system that brings mountain water to eight million people. You will be surprised how good it is, and amazed that so many people could receive it so freely. Similarly in the arid land north of Jerusalem our Teacher spoke to a woman who was having to deal with well-water laboriously obtained. Ask me, he said, and I can give you living water. It is the best water in the world, and there is enough for everyone. And it is just what you need to live. The human animal, who is 90 percent water, who lives on the planet that is 70 percent covered with water, can drink the living water of the Teacher and live richly, live for ever.

Night

WHEN I WAS A SEMINARIAN in the early Eighties, Citibank, proud to be the first with automated teller machines, had a tagline in its advertisements: "The Citi never sleeps." Times have indeed changed. Today even in Woodward, Oklahoma, you can do your banking at 2 AM if you want to; yet it remains distinctive of the City that it sleeps not. You can get a hot pastrami sandwich anytime you want.

My gym isn't open 24/7, but it does open at 5 AM on weekdays. So occasionally I'm walking to it at that hour—and what life there is: delivery trucks unloading, hoses out as guys powerwash the sidewalks, garbage trucks gathering the remains of yesterday, taxicabs trolling for early rides to the airport. A couple of people are inside Starbucks preparing for their first customers. (This is true of *both* Starbucks in the five blocks between my home and the gym.) The free daily papers have already been dumped by the subway entrance. Traffic is light; I needn't wait for green lights. And of course (for much of the year) it is dark.

In a sense, even our choir school never sleeps. We have someone at the front desk throughout the night, as we do through the day, primarily to protect our boys. I ask Ron, who works some of our nights, how it's going. He likes to watch the monitor for the security camera on the street. Pretty quiet, he says, although (he chuckles) there were some interesting people who came by just after the bars closed at four.

One night I went out with my son, Michael, at 11 PM to get a latte, and we walked a bit on the near end of Central Park. "Is that a star?" I said, looking to a point between the trees. We think it was. How different from the mountains of northern New Mexico, where Susan grew up, where on a clear night (and most nights are clear) the whole pitchblack sky is punctured with pinholes of light. Especially when the moon is absent, you can see how great the variation is from star to star. Some are just specks, like glowing dust, while others are large and flickering things which have points as you look at them. There are thousands upon thousands of stars, but each is different from the others in the mountain sky.

Yet in the city, you aren't even sure if the one you can see is a star. "It's not moving," Michael said, so we knew it wasn't a plane or a satellite. It might have been a planet, though.

A few times when I was in college I visited the Monastery of Christ in the Desert outside Abiquiu, New Mexico. From Santa Fe, it's an hour's drive up into the mountains on paved highways, then another hour for the final thirteen miles along a dirt road that hugs the side of a deep mountain valley. (You start talking to God right there, hoping to avoid meeting any oncoming cars on the sharp, narrow turns.) Christ in the Desert is a beautiful, isolated place, in those days without ordinary telephone contact or other quotidian communication with the rest of the world. Invited to join the monks' daily life, we rose at 4 AM to pray (walking to the chapel under all the stars of heaven), had other prayer hours through the day, did some field work, had two meals, and said Compline and went to bed just after 8 PM. It was the only time in my life that noon was the true middle of the day. The monks' life was synchronized with the praises of the heavenly spheres.

The city needs that and sometimes we suffer its loss. But heaven, I am reminded, comes down to earth as God's end-of-time gift, not in the form of unpolluted nature, but as a city. Jerusalem—the city of God's peace—will be itself a place reconciled with the stars.

Smells

THE CITY IS RICH in many things, including its smells. It has many more of them than small towns and suburbs, which are rather antiseptic by comparison. I grew up in a small "city" of ten thousand souls in northwestern Oklahoma. We had front lawns and back yards; everyone did—rich, poor, it didn't matter. Behind the back yard was an alley. Trash cans were in the alley, and the garbage was collected there, once a week. Consequently, except when you were taking it out, you never smelled the garbage. Out of sight, out of nose.

But not in the city. Garbage has to go on the sidewalk—where else could it go? And it can hardly wait indoors for a whole week before going out. So every day is garbage day: every day you find garbage bags on the sidewalk, piled here and there. A further complication, adding to the smell, is that hungry people rip open the bags to glean what they can. This happens particularly to the bags in front of the grocery on our block, but I've seen it also in front of the bagel café. So in the warmer seasons, the garbage smell becomes ripe and strong.

There are pleasant smells as well. Around the corner is an Irish pub—I've never been inside on account of its high decibel content, but just outside the door, when you walk under its air conditioner, you get the luscious aroma of grilled hamburgers. Baked bread is another smell; I love it so much I've occasionally taken a detour so that I can smell it as I walk by. Occasionally one encounters the smell of chocolate or pastry. A sort of hippie sandwich place on 55th somehow manages to get the smell of soup outside its door. And coffee! Let me tell you about the smell of coffee.

I remember back in seminary days, when we lived in a student apartment in Chelsea without air conditioning and thus often had our windows open, that it seemed every morning we got waves of coffee smell. In reality, I have no idea where this smell came from or what it was. But in my mind, it came from a giant coffee grinding factory just across the Hudson in New Jersey, where they were preparing all the coffee for all the commuters who had to cross the river that day. Every morning, tons of coffee beans were turned to small granules, and up up up went the tiny particles with the wonderful smell, which was carried by the winds over the river and then lovingly scattered across Manhattan.

Besides food smells (real and fantastical), the city has people smells too, particularly in a packed subway car or a crowded bus; some are pleasant, others not. And there are machine smells: the diesel of a truck, the engine oil smell of the exhaust coming from the side of a building. There is the dank smell, slightly moldy, coming up from the subway track while you wait in an out-of-the-way station. In the parks, or in a springtime basket outside a window, one can smell lilac or humus or tree-blossom. And in more places than you would expect you can be surprised by urine smell: in a corner, along a wall, beside a gate.

I can think of only two strong smells that I have not encountered in New York. One is a country smell, yet some other cities have it: that of the feed-lot. Drive past one with two or three thousand cows, as you can a few miles outside Amarillo, and you'll be sure your windows are rolled up. The other is the smell of sulphur, which is sometimes near oil or gas wells.

Still I think it is fair to say that cities are where we find the richest combinations of smells. That is part of their gift, an aspect of the riches that they bestow upon us. We city folk cannot avoid the smells of our world. From our food to our garbage, from the smells consequent to human engineering to those that come from the earth, hundreds and hundreds of smells are ours here in the city. And it makes me wonder why God created smells. They are strange things, after all. We might get along without them. But God didn't want to create a dull or simple or just-good-enough world. He wanted to create a world rich with variety and surprise.

Smells are part of the variety and surprise of the city. And since we are human all the way, smells must be part of the surprise of heaven.

Sounds

IT TAKES A DRASTIC ACT of nature to turn the city silent. Shortly after Father Mead called me to Saint Thomas, we had a weekend blizzard with some eighteen inches of snow. Sunday morning, the city belonged to the people. Cars were buried, the plows were not yet working, and you could walk down the middle of Fifth Avenue as if you owned it. Human voices, here and there; the scraping of a shovel; a shout, a laugh, and the rest was silence.

Apart from a serious snowfall, it's cacophony 24/7. Trucks delivering goods or taking trash away. Buildings sheathed in black netting being gutted and then jack-hammered to rubble. The squeak of the brakes on the bus pulling to its stop, and then the warning beep as it "kneels" to let on passengers. And the honking.

I have strong views on honking. At 60th and Amsterdam, beside Fordham University and down the short block from the Time Warner Center, there is one of those signs that say "No Horn Blowing Except for Danger." It is a peculiar sign, for it raises the question, Why else should you honk except when there's danger? Yet the reality of city sounds is that most honking comes from drivers who are impatient; they want the vehicles in front of them to *move on*.

One rainy afternoon we were getting out of a taxi at the parish house on 53rd; there was no place to pull over, the sides of the street being filled with parked cars and trucks. As we were getting out, a process which for Susan is also very slow, the cab just behind us made me jump with a sharp and long honk. I reached Susan's door and, holding up her cane, shook it at the honking cab. What did he want us to do?

Such harshness and impatience marks many of the sounds of the city—I could add the piercing whistles of the Hilton's bellboys—but fortunately they are not the whole story. Recently I was walking down Sixth and I heard a television broadcast of a sports game (basketball, I think). It was amazingly clear, as if I were in someone's den sharing a beer. I turned and saw I was walking past the offices of a cable network. Two men, who were going parallel to me for several blocks, were discussing the use of "members' money" and the unreasonableness of a $400 bottle of wine. A woman whom I pass, who was loudly weeping, was telling her cellphone that this wasn't a good time to talk about "it." Others were talking to invisible cell phones—if they weren't just crazy and talking to themselves.

We have about eight million human sounds here, each with a distinctive voice. We also have music. You know how good your voice sounds when you sing in the shower? Try a subway platform: it is wonderfully resonant. Saxophones, electronic keyboards, violins, even the unaccompanied voice; highbrow or lowbrow, it all sounds good. I give extra thanks to subway musicians because, by their presence, they tend to diminish the background noise. Then the train comes in and shakes the ground and you can't hear anything except the tons of metal speeding past you, or squealing to a stop.

Have I heard birds singing in New York? Yes, in the park; I've also heard squirrels chirping at each other, and children's voices, crying and laughing and gleefully shouting. And I've said nothing about the sounds inside buildings: music, rustle, orations, office machines, elevators. As I write this meditation, I hear dimly some honking from the street below, but more constantly I hear the low fan that continually blows inside our heating unit. Some dishes are clinking in the kitchen, and the keys on my keyboard click letter by letter.

The city is a chaos and a cosmos of sound. Millions of voices, multiple millions of places; sounds of edginess, anger, inquiry, commerce, construction and destruction, affection, laughter, and weeping. It was into a world of many words that the one Word came. Can we hear the Word among our many competing words? Can the one true Word sound in our city of many sounds?

I keep hoping I'll hear him.

Spit

I HAD THE EARLY MASS one Lenten Sunday, so I was out walking in the brisk sunlight of a new spring day at about seven thirty. The streets are quiet at that hour on a Sunday: very few cars, some joggers, some tourists waiting for their bus. As I approached the corner of 57th and Sixth, a man rose from the standpipe and moved quickly toward me, lurching at something of an angle. "I need to talk to you." I slowed down but didn't stop, and said what I usually say: "Sorry, I don't have time." He continued beside me, aggressively pushing his story that he just wanted some money so he could get breakfast at McDonald's. I raised my palm and said quietly, "Sorry, I have to go on," and I turned to cross 57th.

Halfway across a street, a juicy gob of phlegm hit me on the back of my head. I didn't stop. I didn't even reach up to feel it.

My strategy for dealing with uncomfortable situations on the street (and I don't think I'm unique in this) is to act with as much indifference as I can, to hope that by moving on I won't fall victim to the danger that I sense. Getting hit with phlegm was a first.

"Well, Jesus was spit upon," I thought when I got to church and was cleaning my hair as best I could. Of course, I also thought, he wasn't spit upon because he refused to stop and talk with a stranger. (And I thought, breakfast at McDonald's would have been cheaper than the cleaning bill for this suit. And I thought, what if he had hit me?)

It is no simple thing, to take seriously the call to follow Christ in our daily life. On the one hand he told us that whatever we do for any person, but especially for *the least of these,* we have done it for and to him. On the other hand, he praised prudence and shrewdness in dealing with the world. *Be wise as serpents, but innocent as doves.*

So we city-walkers who are Christians have to think about the many people who ask for money. What do we know about them? We know that some of them are professionals: they ask for money instead of doing something else because they have found it to be profitable. Begging is, as it were, their job. We also know that some of them have problems of chemical dependency. Money given to them will go to purchase alcohol or other drugs. We know that others have mental illnesses, and are on the street because they are not receiving proper treatment. In all these categories, there may be a fraction who are potentially violent.

We also know that there are those who fall into none of the above categories, who nonetheless have lost their home and have no place to live.

All of them, like you and me, have been created by God in his image. Our faith tells us that there is an inalienable dignity to every human being. Faced with systemic problems of homelessness, untreated mental illness, and substance abuse, we need to work on systemic solutions.

Still, what do we do with the man who importunes us on the street? With each member of our race, Christ, the perfect image of God, has placed himself in solidarity. This theological consideration is what bothered me the most, as I reflected on that early Sunday encounter. I regretted that I had not found some small way to affirm his dignity. I am no romantic: there was nothing I could do to solve his problems, and I had no remorse about not giving him money. Indeed, about his problems, they may be beyond any human cure. But I wish I had recognized him as a brother. Not on account of the outcome: brother has spit upon brother before—and worse. And I do not remove his responsibility for his actions. Nonetheless...

So I got to share with my Lord the experience of being spat upon. And at the same time, I discovered my Lord in the one who spat upon me.

Memory Tricks

A PROBLEM THAT SOMETIMES COMES with age is we start to lose the ability to speak the word we want to say. We've all seen this with others, and perhaps occasionally we see it in ourselves. Susan has a fantastic vocabulary—she still beats the socks off anyone who dares to play her a game of Scrabble—yet she often can't say what she wants to say. But her compensation strategies are themselves brilliant. Perhaps she's trying to say "sidewalk." She might refer to "the road around the building that the cars don't drive on." Even more fun is something like, "You know, where it ends," which would be an allusion to the classic children's book by Shel Silverstein, *Where the Sidewalk Ends*.

These mistakes, in their own way, show us how connected we all are. It is words that make us human beings, more so than our bodies. That's because it is words that connect us with each other and make it possible for us to form models of our lives, artistic representations, the constructs of culture that convey identity and meaning from person to person and past to future. Aristotle defined the human being as the political animal, by which he meant the animal that lives in communities founded on communications (as opposed to instinct). Sin can be understood, profoundly, as the breakdown of communications, the separation and isolation of person from person and, of course, from

God. So when God took it upon himself to save us, it was God's Word that became man. The Word became flesh and dwelt among us so that we could live together as human beings. This means to live in communication one with another. The Word became flesh so that we could use words well and be friends.

Down the street from General Seminary was a deli favored by many students. It was run by a man named Frankie. Even years after you graduated, if you went back to the seminary you would want to visit Frankie's. And if he was in, he would invariably recognize you and say, "How are you, my friend?" He never learned our names, but he always called us friends. I'm sure it was good for business. But might there not be also a suggestion of depth in those words, "my friend"? The Word became flesh so that we could live together as friends.

Demolition Secret

CONSTANTLY, NEW YORK IS BEING REBUILT. Sidewalk sheds, the temporary structures that go over sidewalks while work is done on the building above, seem to cover ten to twenty percent of the blocks at any one time. Buildings are being checked, resurfaced, their bricks remortared. Old buildings are coming down, and new ones much taller rise in their place. A newcomer is impressed but has the idea that, someday, all this work will be over. There won't be any sidewalk sheds, there won't be any demolition. A newcomer says to a visitor, "One of these days, this is going to look really good." But that's illusion: it will never be finished.

When an old building is going to be taken down in your neighborhood, what you first notice is the closing up and moving away of the ground-level stores. Then the apartments above empty out, and the windows darken. Finally the entire front at street level, all the glass and doors and everything between, is boarded up. The sidewalk shed appears. Scaffolding is erected from the shed to the top of the building, and all around. Then black netting is wrapped around the scaffolding, as if the building had died and was now being enshrouded for burial.

You see, they can't do a simple dynamite destruction, when the building they're tearing down has been built smack up against other buildings on either side of it. So it takes great care, and not a little time. The building has to be, literally, de-constructed. All the interior that can be torn out and taken away, is. And then they start at the top, with jack hammers and backhoes, ripping up the roof, then the upper walls, and one by one the floors. The debris is taken down through the building and out a gate onto the street. Gradually the scaffolding and black netting get shorter, one floor at a time, as the building is chipped and crumbled away within.

It takes awhile, this demolition. And during the months it goes on, whenever you walk past the gate at the front of the building you feel an unusual dampness, and you smell the old moisture that had built up inside that building for decades upon decades. This cool muskiness surprised me when I first noticed it. There were a couple of old buildings across from Carnegie Tower on 57th that had taken a year or more to get emptied out. But when they finally started demolishing them, it was like air conditioning, like walking past the opening of a damp cave that I was forbidden to enter. I made sure my summer walks went past there whenever I could.

The moisture, the coolness, the dank smell was a secret that had accumulated inside the old building over the many years of its life. And now it was coming out, like released past time which, if it could speak, would tell us the secret of all it had seen. It was like Grandma's cellar that you visited in the summer as a child, the cool space underground where canned vegetables were stored before they ever had a refrigerator, a coolness where you could imagine lives of people who were your kin, your ancestors, but you had never seen.

Smells build up in churches too. My secretary in Hopewell Junction prized, as a "fringe benefit" of her job, coming in on Monday morning to an office that smelled of incense. That lingering smell which, over the years, sinks into wood and fabric: it's like an almost invisible layer of paint that you keep putting on, so thin you don't see any difference, but you spread a bit of it every week, and after many years it's so thick you can feel it. We have an incense room at Saint Thomas, and it has a similar feel to it, even though we have the window wide open whenever the thurible is burning. I'm not sure Saint Thomas has fully embraced incense.

Smells build up in churches from candles too, their smoke and beeswax rising to the very top and over the years giving a dark patina to whatever is in the ceiling. And other things build up in churches, even less tangible than the smells of incense and candle. The floor gets worn from many feet. Wood gets rubbed in places from hands folded on it in prayer. Kneelers are permanently indented; cushions compressed. Sometimes there are objects of devotion which people have kissed; an old icon, venerated by tradition in a lower corner, may have little paint left there.

You walk past a church on a hot day, and if you are lucky at that very moment the door will open and out will come a strangely cool smell that, if it could speak, would tell you of thousands of people who had walked and knelt and seen and smelt within its walls. But unlike the de-construction site, you are allowed to enter this somewhat darkened building, smell the muskiness, and feel the dampness. It is a refreshing thing to do when you're walking in the city. Come in and kneel in a place (as Eliot puts it) where prayer has been valid, a place where your prayer can rise up like incense, like a thousand candles, a secret in the heart of the city.

Being Prayed For

"UPDATE: CHEST TUBE IS COMING OUT today. Please pray that breathing will improve. He is struggling." A day later: "Dan has taken turn for worse. He is in ICU on ventilator." Two days later: "Holding his own. Vital signs good. Making adjustments to the ventilator, but still headed in the right direction. Keep praying!" Then: "Dan had an okay day today. The vent is now at 70 Percent. Still some fever. May get a TRACH in a day or two. Please keep praying."

These are text messages, brief telegraph-like communications with missing words and odd spelling and capitalization. The sender is letting her recipients know the progress of her husband, who has pulmonary fibrosis and is coming to the end of his ability to use his own lungs. Texting, as we put it in a rather ugly neo-word, is a way to make short, immediate contact with an individual or, as in this case, with several people at once, here spread across the continent. We do not want to be alone. I've mentioned before the line, "Reach out and touch someone," what AT&T used to say to encourage us to use their monopoly long distance. Now we touch with Instant Message.

But notice, please, the repeated content in the messages above. *Please pray.... Keep praying.... Please keep praying.* Prayer too is a way we connect with one another, and it is completely not technologically dependent! It is an old thing, prayer, and at the same time as comforting as anything could be. You're going through a crisis, you're looking for work, your husband is on a ventilator, whatever it is that's happening to you: to know that others are praying for you and praying with you is deeply good. Nothing may have changed in your situation, but now you know you are not facing it alone, not facing it on your own strength only. Others are with you, and together you are calling on God, and it is very good.

I say, it is a common human thing and very old for us to appreciate the prayers of others. Peter Brown, in a lecture on the letters of Augustine, spoke of the concern we find in those letters to know the condition of their recipients. Augustine carried on extensive correspondence with many people all over the Roman Empire. And he was praying for those people, and he wanted to know about them. Were they being true to the faith? Were they being attacked in any way? Were they, indeed, still alive? The connection of prayer, you see, runs deeper than any particular knowledge. Augustine was connected with hundreds of people by letter. But a letter in the fourth and fifth centuries could take months to reach its recipient, could perhaps never arrive, or a letter in response could itself be lost. The connection given by prayer longs for knowledge and information. But it is a deeper connection. Prayer runs deeper in our being than anything we can know, anything we might poke out in an Instant Message.

We humans are social beings. When we first appear in the Bible, in the first chapter of the first book that happens to be called Genesis, we appear in the plural singular. God made man, the text says; and right away it says *male and female created he them*. Humans aren't individuals that come together to make societies. It's the other way around: there are societies out of which individual humans emerge. So we talk, we reach out and touch each other, we do (or some of us do) rather odd things like texting, because we are social. Most of all, we pray.

This is true even for Jesus. In the seventeenth chapter of John, at the conclusion of the long discourse Jesus has with his disciples at the last supper, you will find a prayer that Jesus makes for his disciples. He prays to his Father that these people would be safe from the world, that their unity would not be lost, that they would be true to the name he has given to them, that the Father's purposes for them would come to fulfilment. The content of that prayer is powerful, of course; but, think about it, it's not only the content, it's the fact that Jesus is praying for his disciples. It's a prayer that he extends to us. Even today, indeed every day, seated as he is at the right hand of the Father, Jesus still intercedes for us, he remembers us in prayer. And why does Jesus do that? Is it because he is God that he prays? Not, I think, in the first instance. Rather, Jesus prays because he is human just like us. Descartes thought the most indubitable proposition in the world was "I think, therefore I am." But perhaps it should be "I pray, therefore I am." Prayer is the heart of our humanity. We have a hint of that when we pray for others, and we have the assurance of that in Jesus who is forever praying for us.

Asking God for Stuff

WHEN I WAS LAID UP after surgery, I read your book." She had come up to me in coffee hour to tell me this. "I've been an Episcopalian all my life, and I never knew you could talk to God, in your own words. Thank you."

Perhaps it is a danger of having such an excellent Prayer Book, that we infer that all prayers need to be as eloquent as Cranmer's. And it is good to have some of those prayers memorized. I sometimes think our rector has the entire Anglican liturgical tradition committed to his memory. At vestry, at breakfast, before a crowd, privately, in a variety of situations he is able to summon up just the right collect for the moment at hand. Our headmaster is similar. He once surprised me by saying that he required boys to select and memorize three prayers before being confirmed. "It's good to have prayers memorized," he said.

I agree, but my assent is more theoretical than actual. There are a lot of prayer fragments that float around in my mind. Once before Evensong when, as the officiant, I was leading the prayer with the choir and clergy, I asked God to deliver us, "as we draw nigh unto thee, from coldness of mind and wanderings of heart," a scrambling that caused John Scott to enter the procession with a smile.

Memorized prayers become part of our soul, and they can emerge into consciousness at times unbidden. This can happen as well with a Psalm or a hymn. Suddenly it's there, you're thinking it, you're saying it through, and you wonder where it came from. You might not have thought of that line or verse for years, but often it turns out to be quite appropriate to your situation at that moment. Dreams can work this way, and we moderns tend to attribute such actions to our "subconscious," although I think it just as defensible to say that God uses our dreams and our subconscious to bring things to our attention. In any event, a memorized prayer is something like a gift to yourself for your future. It is a tool stored in your memory, waiting to be retrieved when needed.

So there is a place for the elegantly crafted prayers of our tradition, a place not only in liturgy proper but in smaller informal settings, and even in private. Nonetheless, prayer is in fact nothing else than speaking to God, and you can do that in your own words. Prayer is talking to God in exactly the same way you would talk to someone else.

We know the intellectual difficulties. God is not just "someone else"; God is our maker, our redeemer, even our judge. As maker, there is a sense in which God is *not* a being; he is the cause of beings and so cannot himself be an item in the universe. How do you talk to the unknown cause behind all other causes? God, as maker of all, must be omniscient, and so he already knows what I will say, he knows everything; why talk to him? God also must be beneficent to the highest degree, and so he already has in mind the good of all things. Why should I speak to him about something that's bothering me, when it must already be for the best from his point of view? And God as the cause of things cannot himself be caused by anything. Thus God never changes. So how could he change as a result of my prayer?

Aquinas says that God is the cause of our free actions. And there is the key to prayer. Prayer is our free offering of talk with God, and even though God causes our prayer (because God causes everything that exists), God's causing it does not take away its free character. This is a paradox, but it's rather like the paradox of light being a particle and a wave. We can't picture it, but it's not a contradiction.

So the intellectual problems of prayer should not keep us away from it, any more than our shortcomings in eloquence. And what should prayer be about? Here is our third line of resistance to prayer. We think it should be about elevated things, spiritual and holy matters. But this is not true. The answer to what prayer should be about may shock you; it shocked me when I first heard it. I once asked Brian how Aquinas defines prayer. Brian's answer was: Prayer is asking God for *stuff*.

Just asking God for stuff?

Well, how about a new car? A winning Lotto ticket? An end to my shoulder pain? A sharper memory? An ability to read books as fast as I buy them? How about an end to Susan's post-brain-tumor problems? A parish without gossip? Lower taxes, cheap oil without environmental problems, and brilliant congressmen?

For all these things, the answer is they might be what you should pray for. I can't repeat it too often: we should pray for whatever it is that we really want. In a sense it doesn't matter what we pray for, or whether it's egotistical, or just, or even loving to others. Because in prayer we are talking to God. In our own words. And once that gets started, there's no telling what God may do with us.

How Can They Go On?

I CAN REMEMBER WHEN MY FATHER DIED," he was telling me. "I was still at home, going to school. It was Sunday night. We had our usual dinner together at home, although he couldn't eat, the disease was so far gone. We had him at home so he could die at home, and that night he did.

"The next morning I went into my parents' bedroom. His body, of course, had been taken away, and the room was tidied a bit, and terribly empty. Despite it being a school day, I was staying home. I went to the window and looked out, and I remember thinking, as I saw other children walking with their books and going off to school, 'How can they go on?' The most awful thing had just happened in my life—my father's life had ended—and there they were, going on with their life as if nothing was different about this day. Outside the window life was going on like normal. Inside, life had ended."

That's how it is when death happens. Your life comes to a complete halt. Whatever is on your calendar for the next several days, you won't be doing. You won't go to school, not to a theatre, and unless absolutely necessary not to work or market. Even the normal inside-the-home routines will be suspended. You may not have to cook, if friends bring food over. Instead of all the usual things, there is a set of extraordinary tasks before you. People must be told of the death. A burial service must be scheduled. The final resting place of the body or the ashes needs to be arranged. There are the loose ends of life: practical, financial. The will must be read, if one exists. Accounts must be sealed, or re-registered. Clothes, papers, souvenirs, hobby crafts, artwork, the hardware and software of life: all the things we leave behind when we die, they must be attended to, distributed or filed away, touched and passed on.

During those first weeks, probably without your noticing, life re-acquires gradually its normal rhythm. The funeral ended, the out-of-town guests departed, you start to take up again your own work, your own routines. After a while you get a handle on what must be done to settle things, and you seem also to get a handle on your emotions.

But from time to time you encounter afresh the original strangeness of it all. In your mind you have climbed again the steps to your father's bedroom. You see the empty bed, the vacuum that has opened up in the middle of things. You feel again the oddness that life outside goes on oblivious to you and your loss.

Except that it isn't odd. It wasn't wrong for his friends to go on to school, to shout to each other as they ran for the bus, to experience the vitality of their young lives. What we experience at death is the intersection of two different sorts of time. One is the ordinary, quotidian time within which we make plans and carry on our usual enjoyments and quarrels. The other is a strange time, almost timeless, lacking the customary successions. It is a time which feels like an infinity that is pressed upon us, leaving us empty, exposed.

Eliot described the Incarnation as the intersection of the timeless with time. But he also, in a famous early poem, spoke from within the mind of one of the Magi after he had worshiped the incarnate Christ and returned home. That birth, he said, was cold and bitter agony for us, like death, our death.

Father Purnell—a larger-than-life Anglo-catholic priest whose sayings are kept alive by my rector—liked to turn the sentence at the beginning of the traditional Anglican burial service on its head. "In the midst of death," he said, "we are in life." I like that too; it confuses our normal sorting of the ordinary and the extraordinary. We live in the middle time between deaths; preeminently, we live between Jesus' death and our own. It is salutary to recall that moment when death came near to us and we found ourselves on the other side of the glass from ordinary life. Both sides are real. Both sides are human. Both have been assumed by Christ, who lived and died for us.

Babies Abounding

I F YOU AREN'T TOO CLOSE, all babies look much the same. Think of the eyes that take up so much of their face, their smooth skin, their paper-thin fingernails. The features of babies are undeniably human, yet they differ from ours in proportion and quality. An extra-terrestrial creature, intelligent like us and yet light-years strange, might seem to us like a mature being dwelling within a baby's body. (And, of course, Steven Spielberg's ET was largely just that.)

Close up, babies are as different from one another as any two adults. Some have hair, some don't; some have chubby toes, others' toes are lanky and long. Their temperaments differ too: this one likes music, while this other one wants to move about. Some are so curious they thoroughly resist sleep; others have a continuous Zen-like calm. They get cranky; they smile. I know one baby who likes being in a car that's moving at sixty miles per hour. Slow down in heavy traffic, however, and she howls. We call it "road rage," and figure she must have come from California.

My daughter-in-law has a sling for her baby. It's about the length of a deacon's stole and worn similarly, over one shoulder and down to the opposite hip. A sling, you see, is a loop of cloth about eighteen inches wide and five or six feet long. The baby lies in this cloth and hangs at the side of the waist, snuggled nicely into a curled, quasi-fetal position. The baby can be lifted to nurse, with the sling then providing a decent cover. I had never seen a baby-sling before, but I am told they are quite popular. They strike me as somewhat hippie-ish, African, low-tech, natural, and brilliant. Sling low, sweet chariot, and carry me home.

For a few years I've been thinking that babies are coming back. One hears the mantra, "Three is the new two," spoken by parents who, if they are New Yorkers, go on about the difficulty of a family of five traveling by taxi. (Most taxis can take four passengers only.) One seems to see more women with gravid bellies walking around. The sidewalks themselves strike one as being pregnant with strollers, many of them with double or even triple seats.

Where are all these babies coming from? A couple of years ago, three women who lived in or were connected with our choir school became pregnant within a month of each other. We had three new babies born, all of them within weeks of Christmas. One theory was that there was something in the water. But I've checked that out, and as a theory it doesn't work, because since those three there haven't been any more babies. Perhaps, though, it was something in the water for just a short time?

More promising, I think, is the theory that babies are coming from people's desire for them. The sidewalks are welcoming to strollers, and so strollers come. Adults are welcoming to babies, and so likewise (even given the taxi difficulty mentioned above). Remarkable things happen when one is out with a baby. You're at a restaurant, enjoying your friends, sipping your drinks, praising the appetizers, ordering, eating, and then, almost at the end, when you're thinking about dessert, the waitress comes to your table and completely ignores you. She's all eyes for the little person in the sling, whose mother has stood up for a few minutes. "I didn't *know* you had a baby there! I didn't *see* her! How beautiful she is!" and on and on. Everyone is happy to see a baby. Even you are happy, even if you never get to order dessert.

I judge it a sign of cultural health for there to be a desire for babies. At the well-spring of our culture is the story of a pregnant woman whose baby was a child of, in a sense, extra-terrestrial origin, intelligent like us and yet light-years strange. He was not, however, an alien inside a child's body, but a divine person who united himself with our human nature. He wasn't *inside* the child, he *was* the child, and he was the man the child became. He remains the most-desired being in the universe. I wonder if it is a step too far to say that he is somehow behind the desire for babies—that desire for babies is in some way desire for him? For it is the case that every human child bears the mark of his having been a human child.

Back Out

IT WAS A SUNNY LATE JANUARY DAY. I had finished lunch with Susan, and I bent over to tell her something, when Twang! it hit me in my lower back. I lay on the floor, I got on all fours, I rolled onto my back; the pain was serious, but I refused to admit it. There had been no back pain for at least ten years. And I had things to do! "I'm going to walk it off," I said to Susan. And so I began to traverse the half-mile of midtown that separates the choir school from the church.

Each tiny step was a study in focused balancing. I walked *extremely slowly*. I walked in perfect straight lines. Jonathan passed me—he was heading back to the choir school following the midday healing mass. *"Are you all right?"* he asked, with his serious pastoral face. Through gritted teeth I asked him if he had raised the dead and healed the lame. And I denied that anything was seriously wrong with me.

At church I could do very little. I tried to sit at my desk, then on my sofa. Then I was lying on my office floor. After a fruitless hour I had to face defeat: my afternoon was lost. I sent a message to the rector that I wouldn't be able to join him at evensong or at class that night. And I went back home.

Walking was now virtually impossible. I hailed a cab, and trying to enter the back seat, collapsed on the floor board in spasms of pain. There I knelt, clutching the seat and the center plexiglass divider, and tried to apologize, and managed to name the address of the choir school. Slowly I inched myself up, pivoted ninety degrees, and eased down.

When I appeared at home, Susan's face was a study in worry. I thought: I'm the one who takes care of her; what would she do without me? She helped me lie down. One of the housemothers came (our housemothers are also nurses). She urged ibuprofen upon me. A few hours passed. Susan went to have supper with the boys, and when she returned I told her I could no longer move myself at all. There was a point in my lower spine where it felt like the whole thing was twisting itself in two. Any attempted movement, and I was screaming.

How could I fall so quickly from healthy normal to utter dependency? "Our future seems endless," I wrote in a sermon about a month later, "and then one sunny day we turn and find we can't get up, and the lights shine in our face, and we pass out of our own hands into others'." The housemothers—I now merited their combined attention—stated that I would have to go to the emergency room. "Emergency room!" I said; "this can't be that bad." They pointed to the fact that I was unable to go to the bathroom. They explained, calmly, that I needed strong drugs to stop the pain-spasm cycles. They reassured me that they would take care of Susan. They phoned for an ambulance. And they started finding things I'd need—some cash, my insurance card—and pulling them together.

A man and a woman arrived. I couldn't lift my head, but when they came near I could see them. Questions were asked; forms were filled out. They pulled me, as gently as they could, onto the stretcher. I screamed. "On a scale of one to ten, what is your pain now?" *A hundred! A thousand!* I was sorry I screamed. They seemed to understand.

It is odd being wheeled around on your back when all you can see is straight above you. The inner ear is not used to experiencing movement from that angle. I said goodbye to Susan at the elevator—all I could do was squeeze her hand, briefly. I felt the elevator's descent; I felt every bump in the floor; I grimaced and screamed when we went outside (now wintry cold) over sidewalk and curb and then the terrifying hoist into the ambulance. I felt, but I couldn't see where we were going. The streets of New York are never smooth; fortunately the hospital was only a few blocks away. I tried to imagine where we were, which lights we'd gone through, which corners we'd taken. Soon I gave up. *My life was no longer under my control, and I had passed into the hands of strangers.*

Back Out II

NEW YORKERS FEAR FALLING into the machinery of hospitals. Douglas, who loves to sing the praises of life in the city of culture and art, invariably adds the codicil: "but don't end up in a New York City hospital." Now it is the case, as I know from being priest or patient (sometimes both) in Poughkeepsie, Kingston, Altoona, and Santa Fe, that people everywhere in the country hope not to enter a hospital alone. You need a friend who is also your advocate, who can keep abreast of what the different doctors and shifts are doing and who can deal with the insurance company, which wants proof that your continued existence for another day is worth the cost. In New York, these burdens of contemporary fragmented medical care are all the heavier because you likely have to bear them on your own. Many people came to the city for anonymity, for freedom from a community that knew everything about them. Others have outlived their spouse or partner or friends. You may be surrounded by eight million people, you may be in the midst of the highest finance in the world and the best music and dance, but fall seriously ill and you are alone.

It even happened to me, and I am a privileged white clergyman living in a community sponsored by my parish. I was on my back with cursing pain, utterly disoriented. I was not in any serious danger of losing my place; I knew where the hospital was and how to get home (I could walk it in ten minutes—if only I could walk!). Yet face to the ceiling I did not know where I was, what street, what entrance to the hospital, what the faces looked like that answered to the voices around me. We turned a corner, then another; I saw now fluorescent lights and ceiling tile.

There was a desk nearby, and it seemed I was being checked in. Someone asked me my name, and another question or two. Then the ambulance man and woman took over answering for me. There was a question about my occupation. He answered: priest.

Now she, the woman from the ambulance, was astonished. "A priest! How do you know that?"

"Didn't you see the books in his apartment?"

He wasn't referring to titles; it was the quantity. He must have seen the four bookcases in the bedroom, the two bookcases that squeeze the hall, the five bookcases in the living room... I used to say we had a ton of books, but that was before our last move. We have thirteen thousand pounds of worldly possessions—six tons—and most of that is books.

Having discovered I was a priest, the ambulance woman seemed to have a new interest in me. This wasn't just a skinny guy with a back gone haywire; this was an exotic specimen. She became a bit more friendly and comforting. I didn't mind the attention.

But soon she and he had to go. I was taken to a cubicle. Someone asked questions. I waited. A woman announced herself as my doctor. She asked more questions, then explained what would be done. I waited. My black shirt was somehow removed. An IV was inserted. I waited. Then a nurse returned. "You're going to like this," she said.

It came in my arm, crossed my shoulders, and slid down through my body. I smelled something sharp and pleasant. I felt happy, like I was floating on a cloud of pleasure. *This is why people like cocaine.* I had been given one unit of something like it—and I couldn't remember what the unit was (a milligram? a gram? a five-pound sack?). And I didn't care.[1]

1 The medicine worked, just as our nurses had predicted. In a few hours I was able to walk around, in a few days it was just a memory. But the medicines! My colleague Father Stafford explained that this is how people like me can get hooked on drugs, trying vainly to recapture the unbelievable euphoria of the first experience when the pain was washed away.

From Complaints to Persons

W E WERE BACK IN NEW MEXICO breathing the cool summer mountain air, exulting under blue skies, and reminding ourselves once again that it really is the Land of Enchantment. On Sunday we re-visited the congregation that had known Susan from her youth (she was not then an Episcopalian, but it's a small town and everyone knows everyone). They knew me because of her, and from our occasional vacation visits over the years.

It is an Episcopal parish and building, but for a decade or two it has worshiped as a combined Lutheran/Episcopal congregation, the two small groups having joined forces for reasons of finance and mission. They alternate, weekly, between the Lutheran and Episcopal prayer books; this happened to be the Lutheran week.

I was glad to be back, glad to be adding a couple of warm bodies to a congregation of, at a stretch, two dozen; glad, too, to sit in an old familiar building too long unvisited. I thought of the summer during seminary when I came back here and did some work. I thought of sitting in these pews with Susan when we were just married. I thought of holding our new baby and standing in the back. And I prayed in thanks.

But such thoughts were lost when we launched into the new Lutheran liturgy. As we sang the first hymn, and went on from that into the Eucharist, a whole string of internal grumblings started to unroll within me. Things like: They've messed up the hymn! They aren't calling God "he"! They're avoiding "Father"! And on and on. If internal murmurings could be picked up by a seismograph, this church would register an 8.0 earthquake. I thought, why must the dear people in a small church in a small town have the latest in political correctness foisted upon them?

But I didn't completely forget myself. I recollected that this wasn't *my* church; I was a guest, and should try to keep that in mind. So I refocused my attentions on what was actually going on, and was particularly grateful to be able to come to the altar and stand beside Susan and receive the sacrament of Jesus.

Afterwards we were greeted by the pastor. "Your name is a familiar one," I said. "Twenty-three years ago this summer, we were living here—it was the summer before my last year at seminary—and our daughter was born that summer. The obstetrician's name was H—."

"My husband," she smiled. He was running a charity golf tournament that Sunday, so we didn't get to see him. Quickly she placed Susan, remembering her parents fondly. And story upon story started coming out, hers, other parishioners', ours. They invited us to a picnic, where yet more people told me remembrances of Susan's parents. Somewhere, for a moment, my mind stepped back and realized that all my unhappiness about that morning's liturgy had vanished. Church life is fraught with anxiety and struggle, and even small far-away churches are not exempt. Yet if the Christian faith is true, then its efficacy does not depend upon us, our liturgical forms, our music. It depends on God.

God had moved me from seeing things to complain about to seeing persons, and he did it in something under an hour.

Thomas a Sign

I THINK A LOT OF US WORRY from time to time that our faith falls short of what it ought to be. We receive, say, a piece of medical news that not everything is right with our body, and we find that we are fearful and worrying. What will this mean for my job? Can I keep working? Can I still go on that vacation? Will I be able to take care of myself? And is there a chance that this is, that this is, that this might be, that I'm coming to —? We fear and worry and then we feel guilty. "If I had more faith," we tell ourselves, "I wouldn't feel this way."

It can also be on the intellectual side, this worry, even for people who come to church week after week for years. We stand and say the Creed. "I believe in one God. I believe in Jesus Christ, God of God, light of light, very God of very God, crucified under Pontius Pilate, suffered, dead, buried, on the third day rose again." We say those words every week, but sometimes there's a voice in our heads that says back to us, "Do I believe that, or am I just saying the words? Do I really believe Jesus was truly God and died and rose in his body from death? Or is it all make-believe; am I just saying the words and ignoring the doubts that are in my mind?"

To think this way, to worry that when we get down to business we turn out to be doubters rather than believers—this is to think of doubt and faith as exclusive alternatives: you have either one or the other. But what if that's a mistake? What if doubt and faith are not like an OFF/ON switch, so that either your faith is ON, and you have no doubt, or your faith is OFF, which means you have doubt? What if reality is more complex than that?

In Saint John's gospel we are told that Thomas was not present when Jesus first appeared to the disciples. When they told him the good news that their dear rabbi and friend, in whom they had placed so much hope, was in fact alive, that crucifixion and burial were not the end of things, Thomas would not believe it. We don't know why he refused to believe, or couldn't believe; it was just there, unbelief. There is a suggestion that he thought the other disciples were always a bit too cheery, a bit too quick to look on the sunny side; there are suggestions, earlier in the gospel, that Thomas was the one most likely to take a gloomy view. "Eeyore" is a name that comes to mind for some people, when they think of Thomas. ("Eeyore" is the loveable but gloomy donkey in *Winnie the Pooh*. Rose, who frequently comes to theology classes here, once laughingly said to me that while other preachers quote the likes of Karl Rahner and e. e. cummings, I quote A. A. Milne.) For whatever reason, Thomas didn't believe. *Unless I see in his hands the print of the nails*—that's what he said.

The next Sunday, one week later, Thomas got what he asked for. Jesus appeared to all the disciples and called Thomas to come over to him. *Put your finger here*, he said, *and see my hands . . . do not be faithless, but believing.* It is the climax of Saint John's gospel. Everything—from the calling of the disciples to the wedding at Cana, Nicodemus, the woman at the well, feeding the five thousand, healing the blind man, raising Lazarus from death, Hosanna on Palm Sunday, washing feet, condemned, hung up, dead, buried, alive—everything has been waiting for this moment. For in this moment, Thomas says something no human being has ever before said to Jesus. It is not given to Jesus' mother to say this, the beloved disciple didn't say this, not Peter, not the man born blind, not Lazarus; it is Thomas, Thomas who doubted, Thomas who says: *My Lord and my God.*

So you see, doubt and faith are tied together in some way, as if *because* Thomas doubted he is able to come to a more insightful faith than anyone else. Perhaps God can use doubt to make faith, the way he uses weakness for strength and folly for wisdom—the way, indeed, he uses defeat on the cross for the victory of new life.

That, I think, is a very comforting thought. And it makes Thomas into a sign for us. The Gospel of John is full of signs, Jesus turning water into wine, feeding the five thousand, healing the man born blind, and many other miracles that John tells us are signs. The great sign that comes at the turning point of his Gospel is when Jesus raises Lazarus from the dead. That seals Jesus' fate, and from there it's a straight line to the cross. But here with Thomas, here on the other side of the cross, is yet another sign, and in a way it's even greater than raising Lazarus. Doubt has been turned into faith, indeed, pretty serious doubt has been turned into deeply insightful faith. What a great sign for us! Jesus came to Thomas and did what he needed so that Thomas was able to have very great faith. It is a sign that Jesus comes to us, wherever we are, whatever the medical news, whatever our questions, and says to us: *Look; reach forth your hand; do not be faithless, but believing.* Even from the grave he comes to us, even when we doubt he comes to us.

Radio Stories

MY DAUGHTER WENT TO CHURCH one Sunday with a college friend. Her friend's church, in Boston, was part of the Lutheran Church–Missouri Synod. After the service they were talking with the pastor, who looked to be well past seventy, and they learned that he had recently been called to Boston from Palm Springs, California. "Wow," they said, "that must have been an adjustment!"

"Not really," he replied; "sinners just aren't comfortable in paradise."

I reared my children on a steady diet of Garrison Keillor's public radio show, *A Prairie Home Companion*. In the made-up town of Lake Wobegon, Minnesota, there are two main churches, the Lake Wobegon Lutheran Church and the Catholic Church of Our Lady of Perpetual Responsibility. Lots of Keillor's stories are about these churches and their people, and my daughter knows most of the stories. So she's always being surprised when real life turns out to be just like the radio. "I couldn't believe it," she wrote me from Boston. "He said it exactly like he was Pastor Inqvest in Lake Wobegon: *sinners just aren't comfortable in paradise.*"

There was another great Keillor story about something that happened to the Catholic priest. Father Wilmer was his name, and he had been pushed over the edge by some parishioners who had installed bright fluorescent lights way up in the high peak of the ceiling of the church. So one night he went into church with his shotgun: he was going to shoot out the lights. He was aiming his gun up there, taking one step back, and then another step, when he felt a touch on his shoulder. That scared him; it was the middle of the night, he thought he was alone in the church, and when he jumped and turned...it was the Virgin Mary. She spoke to him. She said: "You got cornflakes for brains, or what?"

Father left the church without shooting out the lights, but he also never told anyone about the vision. Part of the reason he kept it secret was embarrassment. He imagined some church official investigating this alleged apparition, posing questions to him. "Let me see if I've got this right. The Blessed Virgin used the word 'cornflakes'?"

My daughter also tells me that not that long ago she came into the midst of a heated conversation amongst her friends about how to distinguish a real appearance of the Virgin Mary from a fake one. She tells me that life keeps imitating the radio. It's all true.

Sinners just aren't comfortable in paradise. Part of the pleasure of hearing someone say those words, in the midst of a Boston winter no less, is to recognize how they are true for us too. First, we get to come out of the closet, as it were, and own up to our sinfulness. And we get to say that being sinners is something that keeps staying with us, even though we spend a lot of time ignoring it. And then, to go further, we can smile a bit at the odd fact that, yes indeed, we aren't comfortable in paradise. Paradise doesn't fit us. Give me some snow and slush to fight against, a month with hardly a day of sunshine, cold wind and grey sky. I'll fuss about it, you bet. We might try to live in Palm Springs, or even Hawaii, but we'll never imagine that we belong there.

On the other hand, life can be troublesome in ways that go far beyond harsh weather. You may not have to deal with people who would like to put fluorescent lights on the ceiling of Saint Thomas because "it's too dark in here," but I bet you know people equally persuaded of equally stupid things, people with whom you nonetheless have to work and live. And just when you're ready to pull out your big guns and take aim at the situation, there might be the tap on your shoulder and the words in your ear. The voice of God is not likely to come in the vocabulary you expect, and he might not say anything highly flattering to you. But still he speaks: even in the midst of troubles he speaks to us. "You got cornflakes for brains or what?" That has the authenticity of the voice of God, and they might be just the words I need, first to smile, then to hear.

What Do You Really Want?

IT WAS IN A PRAYER CLASS that the question appeared. We had talked about the various kinds of prayer, about a few simple strategies for making prayer a part of regular life, and of course we talked about the definition of prayer as a conversation with God. I had also said what I think is the best advice, period: that in prayer, we must above all be honest and ask God for what we really want. You may think that you ought to pray for peace in Gaza, but if what you really want is for your toe to stop hurting, and you honestly don't care about Gaza, then pray about your toe. If you try to pray about something that you're not interested in, you'll fall asleep. And so will God.

So pray for what you really want. Be honest before God. And then in the class we all saw it, the question that appeared before us at that moment. You perhaps have seen it too. A man gave the question voice, saying something like this: "My sister was close to me all our life. Even when we lived in different countries, we would phone each other every day to talk. Then she started losing weight, and they couldn't figure out what was wrong, and not a day of her life was free from pain. When the cancer was found, they did what they could. I prayed for her every day. I asked God to heal her; I didn't want her to die. But nonetheless...she died last October."

So there it was: a perfectly legitimate type of prayer, asking God for other people; a conversation attempted with God; complete honesty in praying for what he really wanted. And the end of it: death.

It seems to me that we have to say that although God wants us to pray to him, and God wants us to ask him for the things that we really want, nonetheless, it is also God's intention that each one of us is going to die. There may be one or two people in the history of the world who never died (Scripture suggests as much), but—do I need to tell you the odds? Death is a piece of our destiny.

Let me go back to my basic prayer advice. There is, as you might have guessed, an unavoidable dynamic that occurs when we pray for what we really want, when we are honest before God. And the dynamic is: we are drawn into a position of honesty, openness, and possibility with the one who made us. I'm telling God that I really want my toe to stop hurting, *please!*—or that I really want my sister not to die. And what God says to us is (says to us so quietly that it's a bit under a whisper) *Good. Now tell me what you really want.* It's my toe, it bothers me all the time, I can't get it out of my mind. *Yes, but what do you really want?* She's so special to me, I've never had a friend as close as her. I don't want her to die. *Yes, you love her; but what do you really want?* I don't want to be alone without her. *Yes, I hear you. You don't want to be alone.*

That, I think, is the secret agenda God has when he asks us to pray. He wants to hear us say, "I don't want to be alone." *Yes,* he says, *you don't want to be alone.*

✣   ✣   ✣

Jesus was coming to the end of his life, as he knew well even if his friends hadn't yet understood, so he spoke to them in an image from their familiar language of agriculture. "A grain of wheat"—perhaps he even pulled one out of the ear of some nearby stalk, and held it between two fingers. "If this stays alone, nothing happens. There's no fruit. But if it falls to the ground, and dies,"—perhaps he dropped it at his feet and pushed it into the soil—"then it bears fruit." He was saying to them that the point of a grain of wheat is not to stay alone but to die and be fruitful. He was teaching them that human beings have a similar choice: to be alone, or to die into fruitfulness.

But why would our teacher hold up as a contrast for us—aloneness, or death? We might more commonly think of death *as* the supreme instance of aloneness; when a person dies, she leaves all her connections behind, she becomes a solitary individual who disappears into the Alone. And yet the teacher's personal story was quite the opposite. He had possessed a distant aloneness, but decided to take on himself the task of not being alone. He ventured out to be with us; he came to be one of us with us. No longer alone, he cultivated our friendship. He wanted us to tell him what we really wanted. And we learned that what he really wanted was to love us.

✤ ✤ ✤

And so you're praying for what's so heavy on your heart, for your sister, that she not die. And he says, *Yes, you love her. But what do you really want?* And you say, "It's so hard. I know we all must die, but why her, why now?" And he says, *Yes, you love her.* And you say, "I know that you also died, and your death was so much more painful than hers, and yet here I am, talking to you, trying to talk to you. What is the fruit in this death?" And he doesn't answer. So you repeat, "I don't want to be alone." He repeats: *I understand. You don't want to be alone.*

And then you heard the question, and as soon as you heard it, you knew it was the question you had been waiting for all along. *Are you following me?* Patiently he asked it, and quietly; and he repeated: *Are you following me?*

May I say I like that short sentence, "I follow you." We use it to mean we understand, that we are "tracking," that we are beginning to see where things are going. Jesus wants to know if we understand the necessity of his death. That necessity arose from his decision not to be alone, but to live seeking our friendship. But for him to seek our friendship meant he had to embrace human death: if he was to be our friend in the deepest sense he had to share everything of ours. Friends have all things in common. For you and me, a fundamental decision has to do with whether we close in to protect ourselves from injury, which is the way of aloneness. To live fruitful lives is to follow him in the way that accepts death. Death is not easy, but it is not the last word. In prayer, in honest prayer, we discover we are never alone.

Where's Alleluia Man?

ARLIER IN THIS BOOK I described Peter, the fidgety congregant in the grip of things greater than himself. Over the many months I knew him, his voice at mass just got louder. He not only shouted "alleluia" at the elevation of the consecrated Host—something no one else does, except perhaps the angels, whom we don't hear. He shouted everything. He shouted "And also with you"; he shouted every liturgical response. Even though the midday mass is short, just twenty-five minutes, Peter was now getting up in the middle of it to go to the restroom or perhaps to take a quick drag. When we shook hands at the end, he stopped asking me to pray for his cigarettes. Instead he said, on the gruff edge of the voice left to him, "Father, thanks for saying mass."

And one day he was gone. I learned later that he had verbally abused our receptionist, his voice instantly at its loudest, and his words unprintable. He was escorted out of the building. The word came that, if he showed up at church, he was not to be turned away, but was to be warned there would be no tolerance of abusive behavior. I think he did come a time or two. But it's been over a year now since I last saw him.

To exercise discipline over others should always be a difficult thing for a Christian. And yet those who have the stewardship of institutions must care for their integrity, so that they can continue in their mission. It is part of Saint Thomas's mission to provide a place to pray and have the heart lifted in beauty and awe. We will baptize anyone who asks for the sacrament, and we offer the Bread of Heaven freely and abundantly, nineteen times a week. But we also have to take care that what we offer today can also be offered ten years from now. When people ask me about what size of offering is appropriate, I tell them to give what they can. Then I add the fact that we currently are spending $5,000 *each day* from our invested funds *beyond* what a prudent withdrawal would be. So we are jeopardizing our future by that much, "and anything you can give towards that would be very helpful!"

The same clarity needs to mark our dealings with people who come. We need truly to welcome anyone, even if he fidgets and has problems. It is not our mission to offer the sacraments of salvation only to those who are already saved. It is particularly not our mission to offer what we offer only to people like us. For it is a great delusion to think that we are fundamentally okay and only people like Peter have problems. Nonetheless, our welcome cannot mean indifference to behavior that undermines the gift it is our mission to offer. I think it is the hardest thing of all to say to someone, "If you do X, you cannot come here." Or, if it is not hard, I fear we have lost touch with the Gospel. And yet, discipline is necessary and is the heavy responsibility of those who care for institutions. There is no identity without boundaries.

Once I had had to discipline Peter. I told him that, if he was going to say the Lord's Prayer, he had to say it the right way. He was saying (shouting), "as we DON'T forgive those who trespass against us." I said, "If you want to receive Communion, you must say it the right way." I was concerned that by not forgiving his enemies, he was harming his soul and in Communion might be drinking damnation unto himself, as Saint Paul says (1 Cor. 11). Yet I didn't know if he was capable of whole-hearted forgiveness, all at once. So I just told him to repeat the prayer correctly, or not to say it at all. He grumbled that day as he walked away, but afterwards he said the prayer correctly.

That was a few months before his explosion. Shortly after Peter ceased being a fixture of the midday service, one of the regular guys asked me, "Where's Alleluia Man?" We all felt the silence at the elevation of the Host. I related what I could about what had happened. And then I answered his question. "I don't know where he is. I hope he's all right." One thing was clear. Although Peter was gripped by many things, he was also gripped by God. I hope to see him again in this life. But if that does not come to be, I will be listening for his voice when, please God, I hear the angels sing *Sanctus, sanctus, sanctus*: the voice that's a little too loud, the whole-hearted and unrestrained "Alleluia."

Senior Coffee

WE WERE DRIVING THROUGH NEW MEXICO, down the interstate that winds around the Sangre de Cristo mountains in order to get close to Santa Fe. It used to be our home, Santa Fe, and so we pulled off to make a restroom stop. What beautiful southwestern Spanish accents surrounded us, both in the look of the place and in the voices. I ordered a small coffee. The friendly woman at the counter said, "Since you asked for a small coffee, I'm going to give you a senior coffee. That'll be fifty-four cents."

I appreciate the favor—I think. But "senior coffee"?

It happened again, just a week later, in Guymon, one of the large towns in the Oklahoma panhandle. (It's huge out there, maybe eight thousand people.) Restroom stop; I ask for a small coffee. "That's one-oh-eight," the young man says, and I give him $1.13, looking to reduce the coinage in my pocket. He looks confused and pushes back the three pennies, but as he does so, a woman reaches over his shoulder and silently voids the transaction. I see the words on the screen: "SENIOR COFFEE." "That's twenty-eight cents," he says.

When does it happen, that young people, ordinary people, start looking at you and seeing a "senior"? I don't think I'm there yet, although the extortion racket known as something like the National

Association of Senior Citizens certainly does. One week before my fiftieth birthday—*one week!*—they sent me an application to join. Who told them I was turning fifty? I threw it in the trash, as I did their second, third, fourth, fifth solicitations. They tell me I'm missing lots of great benefits by my refusal to join. But I say, being fifty doesn't make you a senior citizen.

Yet those clerks who gave me a senior coffee didn't ask my age. They just looked at me.

It reminds me of something Bishop Grein once said about priests. There are two words for the word "priest" in Greek. One, *hiereos*, means the holy person who offers sacrifice. Jesus is *hiereos*, and all the baptized participate in his priesthood. Hence you get the phrase, "the priesthood of all believers." The other word for "priest" in Greek is *presbyteros*. This word can also be translated "elder." In the church's three-fold pattern of ministry—bishop, priest, deacon—the person in the second order is a *presbyteros*, a "presbyter." The history of these two words for "priest" is complicated, but the outcome is that what we call "priest" today is an intersection of these two old words. A priest is a member of the presbyterate, and as such a person who offers prayers and intercessions and specifically offers the sacrifice of the mass.

Now as people get older, the range of focus of our eyes narrows, and most of us start needing glasses in order to read. What do the doctors call this condition? *Presbyopia.* Literally, that's "old-person's eyes." Likewise the presbyter, that is, the person we usually call a priest: he is, literally, an old person. And that's what Bishop Grein was telling us. He said we should think of the bishop as seated not alone but surrounded by his presbyters, a bunch of old guys looking wise. We all laughed. We were all younger then.

But what is the old-guy-ness of being a priest? I was twenty-nine when I was ordained. When I think of all the things I didn't know then, I am amazed they let me loose. I didn't know what to say when Sean, age five, slowly died in the ICU. Or when Debbie, a young adult, and her mother came to meet me so that I would know her before she died of AIDS. Or what to say to David, who, when I told him that hell was nothing but separation from God, answered, "So it's not so bad then?" I was young; I don't think I was very effective.

And yet, when Bishop Stuart Wetmore laid hands on me, what he was laying upon me was the burden of the tradition. In that sense, I was made an old man at twenty-nine. A priest is authorized to say mass and pronounce blessing and absolution from sin, all in the name of God who sent his Son to live and die as one of us for the sake of our salvation. And I discovered, as every priest does, that I could be supported by Christ and carried along by the love of people, regardless of my ineptitude. I discovered I was loved, even when I had no words to say, just because of who I was, *whose* I was: a priest of Christ.

Now with a lot of grey in my beard, I guess I'm starting to look the part. But I wonder: did those coffee clerks see just an old guy? Or did they see an old guy looking wise?

Vigil

IT'S 5:30 PM ON SATURDAY, the evening before Easter. The clergy have just ambled down the sidewalk from the parish house to the Fifth Avenue doors of the church—a strange sight for some folks to see people walking in gold vestments down the sidewalk, but hey, this is New York, we've seen everything. Now the doors of the church are closed. Jerry checks the time on his cell phone, and lights a fire in a small charcoal grill. The rector knocks on the door.

What is now beginning is the most dramatic service ever staged in the church. The huge Paschal candle is being lit—this year it's six feet tall. Up the center aisle it is borne, the Light of Christ, as gradually everyone in the pews lights a hand candle. Gregg will sing praise to God for this light, which represents the Light, who was dead but has been restored to us. While he sings I look out over the congregation. Five hundred people, five hundred small candles. Nothing is so beautiful as the human face lit by a candle.

Charles will tell me later of an insight of Michael Bourdeaux, a scholar of the repression of Christianity in the Soviet Union and Eastern Europe. Even when it was illegal to do so, Christians would gather in the night to celebrate Easter, holding candles that illuminated their suffering, lined faces. Each human face is an icon of Christ.

After the singing, five of the greatest stories of all time are read: creation, the flood, the sacrifice of Isaac, crossing the Red Sea, and the dry bones. To hear those stories sound out into the darkness of the church is to be removed from the sense of any particular time. *In the beginning God created the heavens and the earth.... God said to Abraham, Take your son, your only son.... And the Lord drove the sea back by a strong east wind all night....* This is 2008, but it could just as well be 1508, or 908, or 208. This is New York, but it could just as well be Antioch, or Kyoto, or Alexandria.

About an hour and a half after we began, the rector will finally shout the A-word, a cry unheard in church since Ash Wednesday some seven weeks earlier. *Alleluia. Christ is risen.* And as the people shout the ancient response, all the lights will go on, bells will ring, and lusty Easter hymns will begin. It is the first Eucharist of Easter, and the heart thrills.

"What's great about Easter," Mr. Ossorgin's son told me thirty years ago in Santa Fe, "is that every Easter is the same." Indeed, every year we celebrate the one great event that founds at once our religion and our identity: the passover of Christ from death to life. Wherever we are, and whatever the year is, it is nonetheless the same event. Just as every mass is not a repetition of the sacrifice of Christ, but a re-presentation of it, so the Great Vigil does not add another Easter to the calendar, but makes that one decisive passover of Christ present to us once again.

Yet one part of the Vigil is different from year to year, and that is the baptisms. For baptism is unique: as an unrepeatable act, it gives to the one baptized his or her name and eternal identity. We occasionally have no baptisms, and often have one or two adults. But this year we had five candidates: one adult and four children. After the readings but before the lights came on, we clergy followed the Paschal candle to the font. There we met the candidates and their sponsors. They gathered around, Ryan making his promises and the parents and godparents of the others making theirs. Father Mead sang the prayer of blessing of the water while Father Stafford put the Paschal candle into it. As incense lifted in the candlelight, Father Mead blew over the water; everywhere in the church you could hear his breath through the sound system. Then each candidate was baptized, each signed with Chrism, each prayed over that he or she would receive the gifts of the Holy Spirit, and each given a candle. They were serious and joyful, intent and moved. I looked at them with strange awe. Here in the dark new life was beginning.

CPSIA information can be obtained at www.ICGtesting.com
Printed in the USA
LVOW06s0856240114

370831LV00001B/34/P